DRUG EDUCATION LIBRARY

HEROIN

KILLER DRUG EPIDEMIC

By Nicole Horning

Published in 2017 by
Lucent Press, an Imprint of Greenhaven Publishing, LLC
353 3rd Avenue
Suite 255
New York, NY 10010

Designer: Seth Hughes
Editor: Katie Kawa

Cataloging-in-Publication Data

Names: Horning, Nicole.
Title: Heroin: Killer drug epidemic / Nicole Horning.
Description: New York : Lucent Press, 2017. | Series: Drug education library |
Includes index.
Identifiers: ISBN 9781534560093 (library bound) | ISBN 9781534560109 (ebook)
Subjects: LCSH: Heroin–Juvenile literature. | Heroin abuse–Juvenile literature. | Drug abuse–Juvenile literature.
Classification: LCC HV5822.H4 H67 2017 | DDC 616.86'32–dc23

Printed in the United States of America

CPSIA compliance information: Batch #CW17KL: For further information contact Greenhaven Publishing LLC, New York, New York at 1-844-317-7404.

Please visit our website, www.greenhavenpublishing.com. For a free color catalog of all our high-quality books, call toll free 1-844-317-7404 or fax 1-844-317-7405.

Contents

The development of drugs and drug use in America is a cultural paradox. On the one hand, strong, potentially dangerous drugs provide people with relief from numerous physical and psychological ailments. Sedatives such as Valium counter the effects of anxiety; steroids treat severe burns, anemia, and some forms of cancer; and morphine provides quick pain relief. On the other hand, many drugs (sedatives, steroids, and morphine among them) are consistently misused or abused. Millions of Americans struggle each year with drug addictions that overpower their ability to think and act rationally. Researchers often link drug abuse to criminal activity, traffic accidents, domestic violence, and suicide.

These harmful effects seem obvious today. Newspaper articles, medical journals, and scientific studies have highlighted the many problems drug use and abuse can cause. Yet, there was a time when many of the drugs now known to be harmful were actually believed to be beneficial. Cocaine, for example, was once hailed as a great cure, used to treat everything from nausea and weakness to colds and asthma. Developed in Europe during the 1880s, cocaine spread quickly to the United States, where manufacturers made it the primary ingredient in such everyday substances as cough medicines, lozenges, and tonics. Likewise, heroin, an opium derivative, became a popular painkiller during the late 19th century. Doctors and patients flocked to American drugstores to buy heroin, which was described as the optimal cure for even the worst coughs and chest pains.

As more people began using these drugs, though, doctors, legislators, and the public at large began to realize that they were more damaging than beneficial. After years of using heroin as a painkiller, for example, patients began asking their doctors for larger and stronger doses. Cocaine users reported dangerous side effects, including hallucinations and wild mood shifts. As a result, the U.S. government initiated more stringent regulation of many powerful and addictive drugs, and in some cases outlawed them entirely.

A drug's legal status is not always indicative of how dangerous it is, however. Some drugs known to have harmful effects can be purchased legally in the United States and elsewhere. Nicotine, a key ingredient in cigarettes, is known to be highly addictive. In an effort to meet their body's demand for nicotine, smokers expose themselves to lung cancer, emphysema, and other life-threatening conditions. Despite these risks, nicotine is legal almost everywhere.

Other drugs that cannot be purchased or sold legally are the subject of much debate regarding their effects on physical and mental health. Marijuana, sometimes described as a gateway drug that leads users to other drugs, cannot legally be used, grown, or sold in half of the United States. However, some research suggests that marijuana is neither addictive nor a gateway drug and that it might actually have a host of health benefits, which has led to its legalization in many states for medical use only. A handful of states also permit it to be used recreationally, but the debate on this matter still rages.

The Drug Education Library examines the paradox of drug use in America by focusing on some of the most commonly used and abused drugs or categories of drugs available today. By objectively discussing the many types of drugs, their intended purposes, their effects (both planned and unplanned), and the controversies surrounding them, the books in this series provide readers with an understanding of the complex role drugs play in American society. Informative sidebars, annotated bibliographies, and lists of organizations to contact highlight the text and provide young readers with many opportunities for further discussion and research.

HEROIN: THE EVOLUTION OF AN EPIDEMIC

Flowers are generally grown in a garden or bought in a store to give to someone you care about. However, certain varieties of poppy flowers are used for something much more sinister. The *papaver somiferum*—a type of poppy flower—is where the production of heroin begins. From this brightly colored flower comes one of the most dangerous drugs in the world and one that is at the center of an epidemic, or deadly outbreak. Thousands die each year from the heroin that is derived from this poppy flower, and it is a rate that is not slowing. In fact, the death toll from heroin has surged since 2010. According to the United States Drug Enforcement Administration (DEA), "deaths involving heroin more than tripled between 2010 (3,036) and 2014 (10,574)—a rate faster than other illicit drugs."[1]

Tackling this deadly epidemic starts with understanding it—how it began, how it developed, and, most importantly, the dangerous effects of this drug that extend far beyond coming down from the high. Heroin has a long and complicated history from the cultivation of the opium poppy in Mesopotamia in 3400 BC to the appearance of opium's refined form of heroin in the late 1800s. Originally used to treat addictions, heroin became the object of addiction itself. Heroin addiction has seen a number of surges. It all began with the first rise in addiction rates in the early 1900s to the development of the black market (illegal trade) and illegal street dealers in the 1920s after the passage of the Harrison Narcotics Act. Eventually, these addiction rates elevated to epidemic proportions in Vietnam during the Vietnam War. Today, heroin addiction has become a matter of national concern, and officials are looking to new, unconventional ways to tackle the epidemic and save thousands of lives.

Heroisch: The Beginning

Opium was at the center of discussions about addiction as early as the 1800s. The use of opium was often confined to opium dens, where addicts could smoke this drug. At the height of the opium craze, the dependence and addiction to it was such that 22,000 pounds (9,979 kg) of opium was imported from Turkey and India to Britain.

From this addictive drug, another addictive, yet helpful drug can be refined—morphine. In 1803, Friedrich Sertuerner discovered "the active ingredient of opium by dissolving it in acid then neutralizing it with ammonia,"[2] the result of which was morphine. Morphine is still in use today for pain relief from things such as surgery, and this drug is much more powerful than processed opium. In fact, it is 10 times more powerful than the opium it is derived from.

Morphine, in turn, can be further refined by treatment and purification with more chemicals. The result is the drug diacetylmorphine, known commonly as heroin. The chemical company Bayer thought that their new drug—with a name derived from the German *heroisch*, or "heroic"—had potential to treat tuberculosis when it was first marketed in 1898. The scientists who studied the drug probably never suspected that in a hundred years, heroin would overshadow tuberculosis as a public health threat.

From Medication to a Public Health Threat

It may seem hard to believe that heroin was not always illegal. Highly addictive and fatal in large doses, it was made illegal in 1924 with the Heroin Act. Even though heroin is illegal, it is still used today, and the drug that was once believed to be not as addictive as morphine is now a public health threat. According to the Centers for Disease Control and Prevention Foundation, "public health is concerned with protecting the health of entire populations. These populations can be as small as a local neighborhood, or as big as an entire country or region of the world."[3] Heroin threatens the well-being of users and often causes death or an addiction that is hard to break. The effects of heroin are not just felt by the user, either. Family and friends often feel the impact of the user's actions, and the user can unintentionally injure other people while impaired. Heroin use is also dangerous to society. It can tarnish communities, and one way or another, the public often ends up paying for a heroin addict's habit.

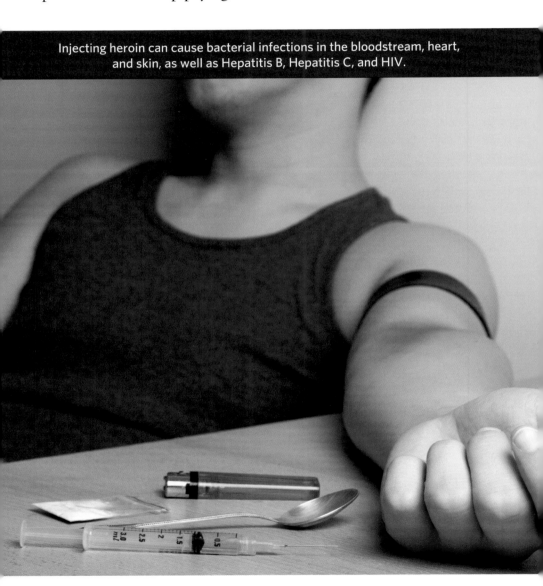

Injecting heroin can cause bacterial infections in the bloodstream, heart, and skin, as well as Hepatitis B, Hepatitis C, and HIV.

Despite these realities, in 2014, there were about 1 million heroin users in the United States alone. What is most disturbing is the number of young adults who use heroin; from 2002 to 2004 and from 2011 to 2013, use among young adults ages 18 to 25 increased 109 percent. Not only is the use of heroin increasing, but the belief in the danger of it is decreasing. Although teenagers believe heroin is the most dangerous drug, "the share of 12 to 17-year-olds who perceive the drug as very risky has declined slightly since 2002 ... Teens also say it is the most difficult to obtain with the share of teens saying heroin is fairly or very easy to obtain declining from 15.8 percent in 2002 to 9.1 percent in 2013."[4] These statistics are disturbing to officials and families alike, and now, more than ever, there is a demand for a reworking of current drug policies, as well as a demand for education and rehabilitation to combat this threat to public health.

Heroin: Deadly Obsession

Thousands of people, particularly young adults, are dying each year due to heroin use. Thousands more are becoming addicted to this drug that can easily turn a euphoric feeling into an overdose. It is a thin line that is often crossed, and many public officials, as well as family members and friends of addicts, are left wondering why. Is it the thrill of coming so close to danger? What is the allure of the drug?

What exactly is heroin, and how does it ensnare so many? Heroin is derived from opium poppies and is sold as a white or slightly brownish powder, or as the sticky black substance that is known as black tar heroin. It goes by many names, especially when combined with other drugs. For example, heroin on its own is known as smack, junk, China white, and big H, among other names. A heroin and cocaine concoction is known as a speedball, while a heroin and methamphetamine mixture is known as a meth speedball. Heroin is dangerous on its own, so mixing the drug with others is even more dangerous and greatly increases the risk of death.

Heroin is an extremely addictive drug and the fastest acting one. It delivers an immediate euphoric rush and the feeling of a dreamlike state. How fast it enters the brain is what makes it such an alluring drug. However, the more someone uses heroin, the greater their dependency on the drug becomes. Unfortunately, with this dependency also comes a tolerance for the drug, requiring the user to use more and more to feel the same as they did the first time. When more heroin is needed to feel the same, there is a greater chance of overdose and death. This risk of death is even greater when there is no way of knowing what the heroin was cut with or if another deadly drug such as fentanyl was mixed with it. This combination of fentanyl and heroin is responsible for many of the heroin-related deaths that officials are desperately trying to combat.

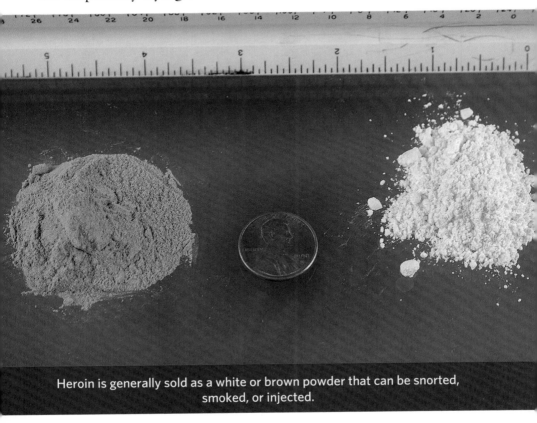

Heroin is generally sold as a white or brown powder that can be snorted, smoked, or injected.

Chapter One

HEROIN'S HISTORY

Heroin has a long history of addiction. While the recent epidemic is not the first, it is by far the most deadly. People have used opium as a painkiller for thousands of years and have been addicted to opium as well. Morphine, which is derived from opium, has benefits as a powerful painkiller, yet again is an object of addiction for many. It was the search for a painkiller with nonaddictive properties and without the side effects of morphine that created heroin. The search initially seemed successful. Heroin was used as medication and even the pharmaceutical company Bayer marketed this new drug to treat coughing in illnesses such as tuberculosis. Once heroin was created and marketed, it spiraled into an object of obsession for many. Heroin addiction does not discriminate between race or economic status. It has been featured in movies, songs, and books and taken the lives of the famous and non-famous alike. What has ballooned into an epidemic and obsession all started with a pretty flower and the search for pain relief.

Heroin's Use as Medication

For about 5,000 years, people have used opium for its properties as a painkiller. One of its earliest descriptions comes from the Greek physician Hippocrates (460 BC), who wrote about the effects of "poppy juice." Opium was commonly used in Europe throughout the Middle Ages. During the early history of the United States, mixtures containing opium were often prescribed as medications for virtually any ailment. Laudanum, a mixture containing alcohol and opium, gained wide popularity. Benjamin Franklin took medicine containing opium for his painful gout, which is a kind of arthritis that causes swelling and burning pain in a joint and is caused by an excess of uric acid in the blood.

Until the 19th century, opium abuse was not considered a social problem. Opium taken orally does not have an extremely potent effect, which lessened the likelihood of a severe addiction or deadly consequence. Gradually, though, the practice of smoking opium caught on. Smoking opium delivered a stronger effect, and addiction rates began to climb. Smoking opium produces the same effect that heroin does—an intense, euphoric feeling. However, just like heroin, coming down from the opium high could be difficult, and the euphoric feeling from the high was so alluring to users that they became addicted to it. In 1803, Friedrich Sertuerner, a German pharmacist, discovered morphine, which is the main active ingredient in opium. At the time, physicians believed morphine would be a nonaddictive painkiller. They also believed it could cure an opium addiction. However, morphine is created from opium, which meant physicians were treating the addiction to opium with a drug that was similar to opium. Morphine was and still is a powerful painkiller, and it was used widely during the Civil War for pain relief. However, doctors soon realized morphine's effects and its addictive allure were even greater than those of opium. After the Civil War ended in 1865, morphine dependency became known as the "soldier's disease."

Shortly after the end of the Civil War, San Francisco banned smoking opium within the city, and this included banning opium dens in an effort to control the widespread addiction to the drug.

In 1874, C. R. Wright boiled morphine over the stove. The result was the first man-made heroin. In 1895, Heinrich Dreser of Bayer pharmaceutical company used chemicals with morphine to create a drug without the side effects of morphine. The chemical name was diacetylmorphine; however, Bayer gave it the name we know today. Derived from the German word *heroisch*, or "heroic," Bayer called its new medicine heroin. The purpose was not to create an addicting drug, nor did the company ever think the drug that was created would be at the center of an epidemic many years later. In fact, the original purpose was the exact opposite—to create the kind of nonaddictive drug that was needed for pain relief.

Bayer's heroin formula was marketed to treat cough-inducing illnesses such as bronchitis and tuberculosis in children. It was made commercially available in 1898. Then, in the early 1900s, the Saint James Society started sending free samples of heroin to morphine addicts. The purpose was a step-down treatment for morphine addiction for those who wanted to quit using morphine. However, once again, drug addiction was treated with a formula of the same drug the addict was addicted to. It is not surprising then that, once again, addiction rates soared. However, for over a decade, heroin use was legal and considered safe.

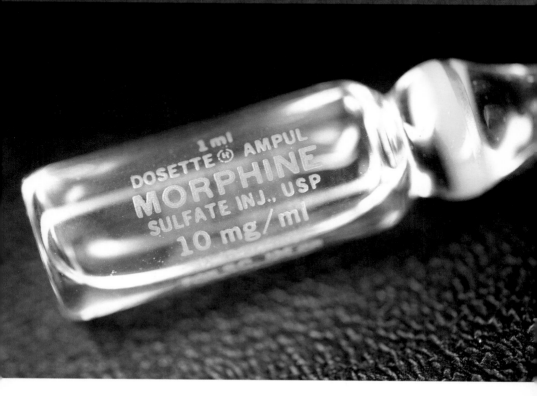

Originally used to treat morphine addiction, people are now addicted to heroin, and it is the cause of thousands of deaths worldwide.

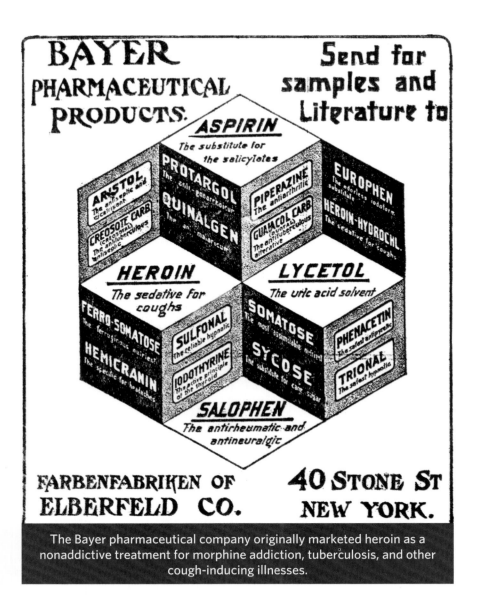

The Bayer pharmaceutical company originally marketed heroin as a nonaddictive treatment for morphine addiction, tuberculosis, and other cough-inducing illnesses.

Production of Heroin

As the abuse potential of heroin became obvious, laws were passed that gradually led to it being restricted and finally banned. Making heroin illegal did not end demand for the drug, however. Criminal organizations took over the production, trade, and distribution of heroin.

The three main areas that contribute to the production of opiates such as heroin are southwest Asia (primarily Afghanistan), southeast Asia, and Latin America. Southwest Asia mostly supplies to neighboring countries as well Africa, North America, and countries in Europe. Southeast Asia primarily supplies to its own area with some of the supply also going to eastern Asia. The supply from Latin America goes to some areas in South America, but these countries primarily supply North America.

Each of these countries grows the opium poppies heroin is made from in remote areas that are dry and warm. Three months after the poppy flower seeds are planted, the bright petals bloom and eventually fall away, revealing an egg-shaped pod. Once the pod is revealed, the farmer makes vertical cuts around the pod. The milky opium sap oozes out of these cuts, and "as the sap oozes out, it turns darker and thicker, forming a brownish-black gum. A farmer collects the gum with a scraping knife, bundles it into bricks, cakes or balls and wraps them in a simple material such as plastic or leaves."[5] Once the opium arrives at a refinery, it "is mixed with lime in boiling water," and then the waste sinks to the bottom while "on the surface a white band of morphine forms. This is drawn off, reheated with ammonia, filtered and boiled again until it is reduced to a brown paste."[6] This paste is dried in the sun until it has the consistency of clay, and then equal amounts of this morphine paste and other chemicals are heated in a container. From this point, the mixture is continuously drained, filtered, and purified until the heroin powder is left.

Different countries supply heroin to different areas of the world, and some of these countries also produce different types of heroin. Mexico provides the sticky black substance known as "black tar heroin," while Colombia provides the fluffy white heroin powder that is generally seen in movies and TV shows. However, the color can vary greatly depending on if there were impurities in the manufacturing process or if additional materials such as sugar have been added to the powder as filler. There is no way of knowing what fillers have been added to the heroin,

Heroin is created from poppy flowers after the petals fall away and reveal an egg-shaped bulb. Opium is derived from this bulb, and then the opium is refined into morphine, which is further refined into heroin.

and it can even be cut with additional drugs that create a more intense high—but at a cost that is sometimes the user's life.

A History of Epidemics

Heroin was supposed to be a nonaddictive drug and one that helped cure an addiction to morphine. However, just five years after heroin was made commercially available by Bayer, addiction rates rose once again. This time, though, the addiction that officials needed to cure was to heroin. Physicians began experimenting with cures for the epidemic, but some of them were quite unconventional. Dr. Alexander Lambert and Charles B. Towns promoted their heroin cure which "consisted of a [seven] day regimen, which included a five day purge of heroin from the addict's system with doses of belladonna delirium."[7] Their cure was not very effective—belladonna is a deadly nightshade plant with side effects that include hallucinations, convulsions, congestive heart failure, and even coma.

After another failed attempt at curing an addiction to one opiate with another opiate, the U.S. Congress stepped in, and in 1906, the Pure Food and Drug Act was passed, which required honest labeling on medications. Shortly after this, importation of opium was outlawed, and there was finally a decrease in opiate consumption.

Although opium was outlawed and heroin was made illegal in 1924, it didn't stop users from illegally obtaining it. In the 1930s, 1940s, and 1950s, heroin was a part of both the Harlem jazz scene and Beatnik cultures. Heroin use was associated with the Beat movement of writers and musicians who felt alienated from mainstream American culture. This included author William S. Burroughs and the jazz artist Miles Davis. Heroin use continued to climb and hit a peak in the 1960s and 1970s with the Vietnam War.

During the Vietnam War, it was reported that 15 percent of American soldiers serving in Vietnam were addicted to heroin, and "the idea that so many servicemen were addicted to heroin horrified the public ... it was thought to be the most addictive substance ever produced, a narcotic so powerful that once addiction claimed you, it was nearly impossible to escape."[8] This inability to escape the addictive properties of heroin helped create the epidemics both during the Vietnam War and in the 2000s. The epidemic during the Vietnam War made former President Richard Nixon take action, and he created offices dedicated to fighting a "war on drugs." Part of Nixon's system in fighting this war on drugs was testing every soldier for heroin addiction. If a soldier was addicted, they were not allowed to return home until they were no longer addicted.

The heroin epidemic during the Vietnam War was concerning to officials and family members alike. According to the National

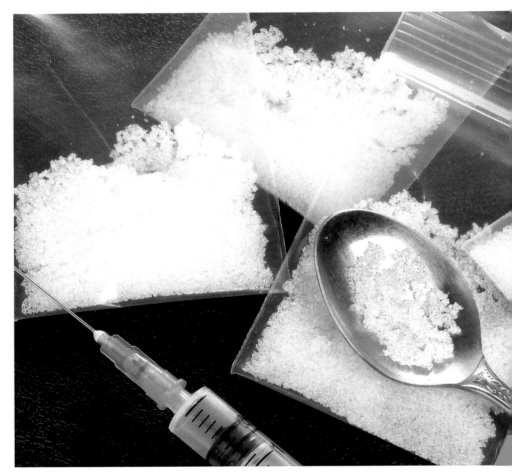

Institute on Drug Abuse (NIDA), "from 1969 to 1974, the number of heroin addicts in the United States rose from 242,000 to 558,000. By the mid-1970s the New York City Health Department was reporting more than 650 heroin-related deaths a year."[9] These figures seem alarming until they are compared with the recent deadly epidemic: In 2014, the number of heroin users in the United States was more than 1 million, and 10,574 people died from heroin-related deaths, making the epidemic of the 2000s the deadliest heroin epidemic to date and also making ending it an urgent priority.

In a survey of teens ages 12 to 17, 20 percent believed there was only a slight risk or no risk in using heroin.

MYTHS OF HEROIN USE

Myth: I do not have to worry about heroin overdose or addiction if I am careful about the dosage.

Fact: The purity of heroin varies greatly, so it is not possible to know the heroin content of a single dose. Assuming that a dose is "safe" can be fatal, and the effects of the same amount of heroin may vary from one individual to another. Also, tolerance to heroin develops very quickly. Regardless of the dosage, most addicts do not realize that they have a drug problem until their drug use is out of control.

Myth: Heroin addicts can stop whenever they want if they just use their willpower.

Fact: Although some addicts can give up heroin on their own, most require help from professionals. Heroin users develop a powerful psychological and physical dependence on the drug. The phrase "quitting cold turkey" has its origins in how an addict's skin becomes cold and clammy due to withdrawal if he or she abruptly stops using the drug. Drug treatment programs can provide guidance and support for recovering addicts.

Myth: Since so many writers and artists have been linked to heroin, there must be some connection between heroin use and creative personalities.

Fact: In most cases, heroin abuse among celebrities best demonstrates how the drug can devastate their lives, not promote their art. The stories of famous heroin users describe tragedy and wasted potential. Although a few personalities managed to live with their addiction—William S. Burroughs died of natural causes at the age of 83 despite a lifetime of on-and-off heroin use—they are the rare exception.

Heroin in the Media

From the beginning, the media did not hesitate to play up the dangers of heroin. In the late 1890s and the early years of the 20th century, there was a sense of national hysteria over opium dens run by Chinese immigrants. Although many Americans were addicted to nonprescription medicines containing morphine and heroin, opium addiction was branded a "Chinese vice" threatening to subvert society.

One of the early opponents of heroin, Richmond Pearson Hobson, fought hard against the media's tendency to sensationalize heroin, so much so that his lectures were often laced with questionable facts and statistics. He started out as an advocate of Prohibition, which was the banning of alcohol. In one speech, Hobson declared that "ninety-five percent of all acts and crimes of violence are committed by drunkards."[10] Shortly after his speech, Prohibition failed, and he had changed his focus: "Most of the daylight robberies, daring hold-ups, cruel murders, and similar crimes of violence are now known to be committed chiefly by drug addicts."[11] Hobson helped convince Americans that heroin use was causing a national crisis. Hobson also argued that "drug addiction is more communicable [easily spread] and less curable than leprosy."[12]

Media coverage of drug stories often intersects with drug references in popular culture. Quentin Tarantino's violent 1994 movie *Pulp Fiction* was alternately accused of glamorizing and misrepresenting heroin use. The movie features an overdose victim being revived by a dose of adrenaline injected directly into the heart. Although it is a dramatic onscreen rescue, it is not a treatment for overdose. The 1996 movie *Trainspotting*, which followed the story of several heroin addicts in Scotland, sparked an intense debate over whether the movie glamorized addiction. The TV show *Breaking Bad* focused primarily on methamphetamine; however, it also featured heroin in some episodes. Jesse Pinkman, a character in the show, was shown going into rehabilitation for drug addiction after the death of his girlfriend due to a heroin overdose. *Breaking Bad* portrayed an accurate overdose scene with his girlfriend passing out and choking on her own vomit.

A celebrity using heroin, especially when it involves a tragic ending, is all over the news and social media platforms for quite a long time afterward. During the early years of jazz music, many musicians were linked to heroin. Saxophonist Charlie

Breaking Bad was a TV show that dealt with many kinds of drug use, including heroin abuse.

Parker and singer Billie Holiday both struggled with heroin addiction. As rock 'n' roll came into fashion, heroin use became associated with the lifestyle of some rockers. Jim Morrison of the Doors, Janis Joplin, singer Nico of the Velvet Underground, Keith Richards of the Rolling Stones, and many others struggled with heroin abuse. During the 1990s, the association between heroin and rock music went through another cycle. Many rockers of the grunge movement popularized in Seattle were linked to heroin. One of the most tragic instances of heroin in the grunge movement was the case of Kurt Cobain of Nirvana, who struggled with heroin addiction before committing suicide.

The Allure of a Deadly Drug

In the past, most people have regarded heroin as the ultimate taboo "hard drug." Casual drug users, who were willing to experiment with marijuana or cocaine, would draw the line at trying heroin. Even some heroin users would draw yet another line at mainlining, or injecting, the drug directly into the bloodstream, especially after the onset of the AIDS epidemic, because HIV, which causes AIDS, was often often spread through the use of shared needles.

However, during the 1990s, heroin began to attract new users: teenagers who did not share the older generation's aversion to heroin. Part of the reason for this was changing attitudes about drugs, both legal and illegal. Heroin may create the allure of danger that seems appealing. However, there is no such thing as just "trying" heroin. It is highly addictive, and it only takes the first "try" to want to recreate the feeling, which eventually leads someone to become hooked on it. Alison, a former heroin user, described how quickly she became addicted to heroin:

From the day I started using, I never stopped. Within one week I had gone from snorting heroin to shooting it. Within one month I was addicted and going through all my money. I sold everything of value that I owned and eventually everything that my mother owned. Within one year, I had lost everything.

I sold my car, lost my job, was kicked out of my mother's house, was $25,000 in credit card debt, and living on the streets of Camden, New Jersey. I lied, I stole, I cheated.

I was raped, beaten, mugged, robbed, arrested, homeless, sick and desperate.[13]

As Alison explained, heroin addicts will often steal items and go to any lengths to get more heroin. Heroin becomes the primary thought and motivator for the addict. Additionally, "the pleasure of the first rush of heroin doesn't repeat itself over prolonged usage. That initial euphoria becomes a lasting memory, and one to be obsessively chased."[14] This means that with the first rush of heroin, the user needs to have that same blissful feeling again. However, the next time he or she uses heroin, they find that the second time does not feel like the first. Nothing compares to the first, and they need to use more to get the same feeling.

Not only does the user stop feeling the pleasure of the experience, but if they use more heroin to try to achieve the same initial euphoric feeling, there is an even greater chance of overdose and death. There is no guarantee of what has been mixed with heroin as filler—it may even be mixed with other drugs such as fentanyl, which creates a more powerful drug. What is in the bag of heroin is a mystery, and one that claims more than 10,000 lives a year. The risk of an overdose is not an occasional one, nor is it dependent on how much you take. "Literally, every time someone injects heroin, they're taking a risk of an overdose,"[15] Jack Stein of NIDA reported.

Even the knowledge that every injection could bring an overdose is not enough to stop an addict. The allure of euphoria and the illusion of a world without problems pulls the addict back to the lethal drug repeatedly. When the addict does try to quit, the withdrawal symptoms are so painful that it leads the user right back to an even more dangerous world of addiction.

THE TRAGEDY OF KURT COBAIN

One of the most tragic deaths that is still mourned by rock and grunge fans is that of Kurt Cobain of Nirvana. Cobain struggled with heroin addiction for years and admitted to the press that he used the drug. The extent of his use, however, he was not truthful about. He told the press his habit was small. In reality, he was buying heroin every day. At one point he had "bought and used so much heroin that the dealer refused to sell him any more."[1] He continued to spiral further into addiction, caught in the allure of drugs.

On April 8, 1994, Cobain was found dead in his home at the age of 27 from suicide. Bandmate Krist Novoselic later recalled seeing Cobain "out of his mind on heroin"[2] a few days before his death, and he also believes Cobain was not thinking clearly due to the amount of heroin he had used at that time. Heroin provides an addictive rush that requires the user to need more and more to have the same feeling. However, that amount can often be lethal—the autopsy revealed that Cobain had taken extreme amounts of heroin as well as tranquilizers in a combination and amount that would not have allowed him to live much longer had he not committed suicide.

Kurt Cobain's death shook the music world in the early 1990s.

1. Charles R. Cross. *Heavier Than Heaven: A Biography of Kurt Cobain*. New York, NY: Hyperion, 2001, p. 336.

2. Kim Hillyard, "Nirvana's Krist Novoselic Says He Saw Kurt Cobain 'Out of His Mind on Heroin' Days before Suicide," NME, September 10, 2015. www.nme.com/news/music/nirvana-21-1225824.

Heroin lures the user in with the promise of a "rush," warmth, and a dreamlike feeling. However, these feelings do not last—coming down off of heroin involves a crash into a dark low that includes insomnia, bone pain, and much more.

DAVIDE SORRENTI AND HEROIN CHIC

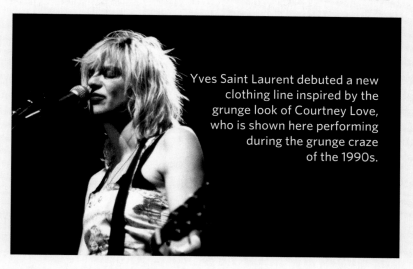

Yves Saint Laurent debuted a new clothing line inspired by the grunge look of Courtney Love, who is shown here performing during the grunge craze of the 1990s.

During the 1990s, the "heroin chic" trend briefly became popular in the fashion world. Very thin models in magazine spreads stared out dully at readers with hollow, dark-rimmed eyes. A notorious ad campaign for a Calvin Klein fragrance featured emaciated models contorted into bizarre positions. The heroin chic look was widely criticized. The main concern with the popu-larization of heroin chic was how the trend glamorized the physical effects of heroin abuse.

Initially, the problem was with the models' appear-ance, rather than with actual alleged heroin use by models. It gradually became known, however, that a number of models had engaged in heroin use. In 1997, 20-year-old photographer Davide Sorrenti, one of the pioneers of the heroin chic look, was found dead of a heroin overdose. Public outcry and censure within the fashion industry ended the popularity of the heroin chic trend until 2016.

In Gucci's spring and summer 2016 campaign, there was debate over whether Gucci was trying to bring back the heroin chic look. *Huffington Post* compared the Gucci campaign with the film *Christiane F*, which was a true story about a heroin addict. They found numerous comparisons "from the settings to the lookalike casting."[1] Additionally, in 2016, brands such as Yves Saint Laurent debuted new looks during Paris Fashion Week that were inspired by the grunge look of the 1990s, which Courtney Love popularized. Love was a heroin addict at one time and was married to Kurt Cobain. These fashion shows and ad campaigns have occurred during the height of a heroin epidemic, which caused backlash similar to the backlash in the 1990s. Drug Abuse Resistance Education (D.A.R.E.) joined the nonprofit organization Heroin Is Not Chic in a campaign to stop the glamorization of the drug and promote awareness of the heroin epidemic. The campaign launched during New York Fashion Week in September 2016.

1. Rosy Cherrington, "Is Gucci Trying To Bring Back Heroin Chic In Their Spring/Summer 2016 Campaign?," *Huffington Post*, January 19, 2016. www.huffingtonpost.co.uk/2016/01/19/gucci-spring-summer-16-christiane-f_n_9017560.html.

Chapter Two

THE EFFECTS OF HEROIN

After taking a dose of heroin, the user quickly feels the "rush" take hold of the body and brain. The drug often delivers an immediate sense of overpowering euphoria, which leads to a pleasant, dreamy state. Some people describe it as a kind of trance, while others say that it makes them feel like all of life's worries, anxieties, and stresses are suddenly gone. Heroin can be taken in a variety of ways—from smoking to inhaling—with effects being felt immediately when it is injected.

Along with addicts using heroin in a variety of ways, the effects of heroin can vary greatly from one user to another. Some users experience negative things such as nausea and vomiting immediately instead of the euphoric rush that makes heroin alluring to users. Although the euphoric effects are alluring, there are many negative effects that happen shortly after using heroin, and these effects can last months or years, changing the user's brain in the process.

The Physical and Mental Effects of Heroin

Heroin can be inhaled, smoked, or injected. Injection delivers the quickest and most dangerous response—within seconds, the user feels the effects. It is also easier to overdose while injecting heroin than by inhaling or smoking. When inhaled, it takes about 10 to 15 minutes before effects are felt. Once heroin is taken into the body, it delivers an intense feeling of happiness that some users have said is like being "covered in a warm blanket, where worries are gone."[16] Along with this intense euphoric feeling, heroin slows things down. The user feels as if they have no problems, their limbs feel heavy, and they also feel relaxed and tired. This effect is what is commonly referred to as "on the nod." However, with the feeling of everything around the user slowing down as they become relaxed, heroin also slows down important body functions such as heart rate and breathing. This becomes especially dangerous if the user falls asleep, as sleeping shuts down the respiratory drive. This means if the user takes too much heroin and then falls asleep, there is an increased chance of overdose and death. According to Dr. Karen Drexler, "when you are sleeping, your body naturally remembers to breathe. In the case of a heroin overdose, you fall asleep and essentially your body forgets"[17] to breathe.

The effects of heroin generally last between four and six hours. However, the effects heroin has on the body and mind make it alluring and necessary to have more. The pleasure center of the brain constantly wants more, but when the user does what is wanted, the pleasure center may not activate as much as it did the first time. The user then needs more and more, and the drug becomes inescapable. As higher doses are added to the user's body, tolerance and dependence soon follow. This may occur over an extended period of time; however, many users go on a binge and use the drug repeatedly to keep the high. Unfortunately, the brain and body cannot keep up.

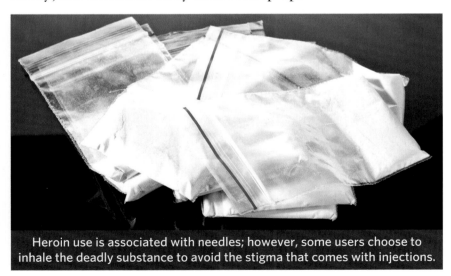

Heroin use is associated with needles; however, some users choose to inhale the deadly substance to avoid the stigma that comes with injections.

Heroin creates a feeling of euphoria that is alluring. However, the body builds up a tolerance to the deadly drug, which requires the user to abuse more and more heroin to achieve the same effect and avoid the loss of interest and depression that follow because of withdrawal.

DETECTING HEROIN

Many companies, as well as the federal government, require that their employees submit to drug testing at the workplace. The reasons are obvious. Drug use can undermine an employee's reliability, productivity, and overall health. In some occupations, an employee impaired by drug use can be a public safety hazard. Some employers refuse to hire people who have any sort of criminal drug record.

Hair, blood, and saliva can all be tested to determine drug use, but urine testing is the most common. Traces of heroin remain in urine for up to two days following use, and an indicator unique to heroin remains detectable for five to six hours after use. Opioids such as methadone do not yield a positive test, and the school or company would need to run a special test for methadone which is not common. The results and window of time that heroin use will be detected depends on a variety of factors. Factors such as height, age, weight, and the drug purity and quality can all affect the window of time that heroin is detectable for.

Certain tests can detect heroin for up to seven days; however, a hair follicle test detects heroin for the longest span of time. While many factors can interfere with the results of a hair follicle test, it can generally detect heroin use within three months.

Department of Health
BUREAU OF HEALTH FACILITIES AND SERV

DRUG TEST

pplication for Accredita   of Drug Testing Laboratory
ame of Laboratory1 :___
ddress of the Laboratory .
o. & Street Barangay

Hair, blood, saliva, and urine can all be tested by schools, hospitals, and employers for the presence of heroin and other drugs.

When a person eats their favorite food, a group of nerve cells in their brain called the nucleus accumbens gets flooded with dopamine. Their brain connects the food with something they are doing for survival, and the release of dopamine is responsible for some of the pleasure that they get from eating their favorite food. This same area gets flooded with dopamine when someone injects heroin, but the effect is stronger on many levels. Heroin floods the brain with dopamine faster, and the effects also last longer. How does taking heroin trigger this "hit" and other resulting effects? Once it enters the body, heroin is converted back into morphine. Upon reaching the brain, opiates affect the central nervous system, which impacts both physical and psychological functioning. The surge of euphoria, dulling of pain, and other sensations associated with heroin use is caused by the activity of nerve cells in the brain. Heroin works by binding to mu-opioid receptors, which neurotransmitters also bind to in order to regulate feelings such as pain or happiness. Opiates bombard the receptors, and the resultant "rush" far exceeds any naturally occurring effect.

Although heroin and morphine work the same way in the brain, heroin acts more quickly because of chemical modifications. When injected directly into a vein, it reaches the brain within seconds. Users may instead choose to inject into a muscle, called skin popping, rather than directly into the bloodstream.

Heroin has a major effect on the brain that goes beyond the euphoria that typically lures users in. When the user

repeatedly subjects his nucleus accumbens to this narcotic-induced flood, the nerve cells that dopamine acts upon become exhausted from stimulation. The brain reacts by dampening its dopamine response – not just to heroin or cocaine, but probably to all forms of pleasurable behavior, in addition, some of the receptors themselves appear to die off. As a result, hyper-stimulating drugs become the only way to trigger a palpable dopamine response. Drug addicts seek larger and larger hits to achieve an ever-diminishing pleasure experience, and they have trouble feeling satisfaction from the things that healthy people enjoy.[18]

This means that when the user is not currently on the drug, he or she finds it hard to be happy while doing things they used to enjoy, such as getting together with friends or eating their favorite meal. Heroin begins to seem like the only path to happiness.

The damage that heroin causes is not limited to the lack of a dopamine response when someone is doing their favorite activity. Researchers at the University of Edinburgh studied the brains of 34 methadone and heroin users and compared the results with the brains of 16 people who had died at a young age but had never used drugs. The heroin and methadone users had an average age of 26, but some of them had died at 17. The researchers found "that young drug abusers were up to three times more likely to suffer brain damage, than those who did not use drugs. The drug abusers meanwhile sustained a level of brain damage normally only seen in much older people and similar to the early stages of Alzheimer's."[19] The study showed that the long-term effects of using heroin are greater than the short-term withdrawal symptoms that a user experiences: Heroin causes areas of the brain to become severely damaged or die and also prematurely age by 50 to 60 years.

This diagram shows the flow of dopamine to the nucleus accumbens in the brain.

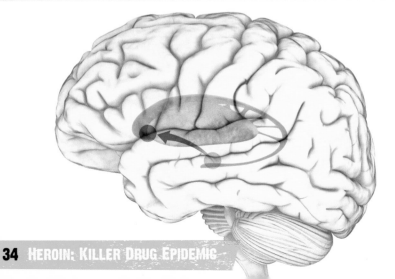

Short-Term Effects

Since heroin affects brain function and the central nervous system controls all of the other systems of the body, heroin use causes a variety of short-term side effects. Heroin makes everything slow down, including breathing and motor skills, and it also causes slurred speech. The initial euphoric rush that is connected with heroin use only lasts for a few minutes. After this, users often go "on the nod" soon after taking a dose of the drug, slumping into a stupor and letting their eyelids droop for several hours. Going "on the nod" happens "because heroin is a sedative, and it can cause a person to go from feeling awake but sleepy into such a deep sleep that he or she cannot be shaken awake. This can seem like a desirable state for a heroin user, but it can be the first step on the road toward excess sedation ... Being on the nod is the first baby step on a slippery slope toward overdosing."[20]

The brain registers heroin as a toxin, triggering nausea, especially for first-time users, and sometimes the user vomits. The pupils of the eyes contract, sometimes to pinpoints. Heroin can cause users to become flushed and develop an abnormally low body temperature. Heroin also causes confusion and sensitivity to light. Additionally, heroin triggers a release of histamine, which makes users' skin feel extremely itchy, as though their skin is crawling.

These effects can last for hours, and those that involve the heart and respiratory system are the most dangerous as these effects can cause an overdose or death. The use of naloxone medication can frequently save people's lives during an overdose. However, it is not meant to be relied on, and it is not a treatment for an addiction.

Long-Term Effects

Chronic heroin use takes a toll on the body. It is hard for the body to keep up while the user is high on the drug, and heroin has equally dangerous long-term effects. Heroin affects the heart and lungs and slows down heart rate and respiratory function while the user is high. These vital organs are also affected from chronic use, and infections in the heart and lung complications may result from extended use. The user may get pneumonia, and tuberculosis—the same illness that heroin was meant to treat in the late 1800s and early 1900s—is also an illness that can occur after long-term use from both "the poor health of the user as well as from heroin's effect of depressing respiration."[21] Additionally, heroin powder or sticky black tar heroin may have additives that the heroin was cut with. These additives "do not readily dissolve and result in clogging the blood vessels that lead to the lungs, liver, kidneys, or brain. This can cause infection or even death of small patches of cells in vital organs."[22] The filler materials in heroin can also cause arthritis, which is joint pain and stiffness that generally occurs in older adults.

Heroin affects the reproductive system, and women often experience irregular periods while on heroin. If a woman is pregnant while using heroin, the risk of miscarriage—when the baby is spontaneously aborted—is greatly increased. If the baby is carried for the standard term of about 40 weeks and the woman gives birth, there is a risk that the baby will be born addicted to heroin.

Specific methods of using heroin also have risks for the user. If the user prefers to inhale heroin repeatedly, tissues in the nose can become damaged. Another consequence of inhaling heroin is a perforated septum. The septum is the delicate bone and cartilage structure that separates the nostrils. With repeated inhalation of toxic substances, "the cartilage begins to die, and a hole develops."[23] This hole can cause "whistling, nosebleeds … infections, nasal congestion, sinusitis, and nasal collapse deformity."[24] When there is nasal collapse, the nostrils can close to small slits and result in the user having difficulty breathing.

One of the effects of heroin is it makes the user feel as though all problems have gone away, including pain, due to heroin being a sedative. However, this effect of heroin can also mask deeper illnesses. As the user is not feeling pain, they may not realize there are underlying issues such as pneumonia, tuberculosis, or an infection, and they may not get the help they need in time.

THE DANGERS OF INJECTION

The most dangerous method of using heroin is injecting it. First, injecting puts large amounts of heroin directly into the bloodstream at one time. As heroin can also be cut with other materials such as cornstarch, dirt, sugar, bleach, or coffee, these materials also enter the bloodstream immediately, and there is no guarantee what materials have been added to the heroin—what enters the bloodstream other than the already deadly drug is unknown. This also opens up the possibility of an overdose and death, especially if other drugs were added to the mixture.

With the rise in popularity of injecting heroin, the recent epidemic has also seen a rise in new human immunodeficiency virus (HIV) cases as well as hepatitis outbreaks due to injecting heroin. The rising new HIV and hepatitis cases are not necessarily from sharing needles, however. Any time any piece of the equipment used to cook heroin—cotton, needles, spoons—is shared between two or more people, any virus can enter the heroin solution. Once this virus enters the solution, it also is injected into the bloodstream, which leads to an outbreak of new HIV and hepatitis cases in a heroin epidemic.

Injecting heroin also has a number of risks associated with it such as skin popping, deep vein thrombosis, abscesses, and collapsed or blown veins. Skin popping may happen by accident or on purpose—the user may miss the vein and hit muscle instead, which still allows him or her to get high, or the user may choose the muscle over the vein for a delayed reaction and the avoidance of the "track marks" that are associated with heroin use. Deep vein thrombosis is when a blood clot forms in an area such as the legs. These blood clots can travel to the lungs and block blood flow, which can be life-threatening.

When a heroin user chooses to inject, or "mainline," the drug, there is a risk of collapsing the veins that are being used. A vein can collapse from the needle being inserted too many times, which causes blood to leak outside of the vein; the vein can no longer be used for injecting heroin or even drawing blood at the doctor's office.

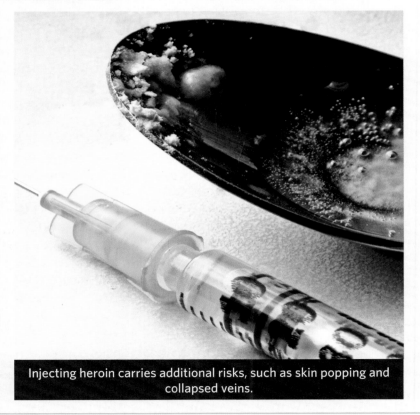

Injecting heroin carries additional risks, such as skin popping and collapsed veins.

Death and Overdoses

When heroin is purchased on the streets, the user has no knowledge of what fillers are added to it, and there is also no knowledge of what other drugs have been added to the mixture. When other drugs are added, it increases the likelihood of an overdose and almost guarantees death. In the recent epidemic, drugs such as fentanyl have been added to the heroin powder. According to John Flickinger of the DEA, "Synthetic fentanyl is approximately 30 to 50 times stronger than heroin and it's deadly … The equivalent of three to five grams of salt of fentanyl is a lethal dose."[25] When this small amount is added to heroin, it has devastating results for the user and their friends and family.

However, heroin does not just have to be laced with additional drugs to turn it into a deadly substance:

> *A heroin overdose happens because use of the drug alters the neurons within every addict's brain—but the alterations occur in different parts of the brain at varying rates of speed. The pleasure center, increasingly hard to satisfy, is screaming "More!" But primitive centers that control breathing and heart rate are not building up tolerance at the same pace and are whispering "enough."[26]*

The body struggles to keep pace with the toll heroin creates on it. However, at any dosage, the heart and respiratory system slow down. At high dosages, the brain is being hijacked by the sedative heroin, and eventually the body forgets to breathe and body systems shut down, which results in death. Studies also show that "tolerance to the depressive effects of opiates increases at a slower rate than tolerance to the euphoric and analgesic effects. As your tolerance to the drug develops, you typically need more of it to produce the high you are used to getting. This may be why long-term users are potentially at a greater risk of overdose than [new users]."[27]

The signs of an overdose occur across multiple body areas and systems including the lungs, mouth, heart, skin, and nervous system. The user's tongue may change color, their pulse may be weak, the lips and nails may change color—blue if they have light skin and gray if they have darker skin—from lack of oxygen, and there may be muscle spasms. Additionally, the user's body may be limp. An overdose is not always fatal, and it does not happen immediately. As these overdose symptoms present themselves, body systems slowly shut down. What determines the outcome is how quickly medical help is received.

Removing the risk of death by quitting heroin is not easy for a user, either. Heroin is a hard drug to forget—positive memories of drug use remain, and heroin creates a powerful memory. Withdrawal symptoms can be difficult, and relapse often happens. The trouble with relapsing is the addict may take the dosage they were used to taking before quitting. However, this is the amount the body developed a tolerance to. Once the user is removed from heroin for a period of time, the body attempts to recover and no longer has that tolerance. When the user injects or inhales the amount of heroin they were used to, it often leads to death.

DRUG MIXING

The body has a hard time handling just heroin as it makes its way through the bloodstream. Heroin slows down normal bodily functions such as heart rate and the respiratory system. However, when other drugs or alcohol are added to the mixture, it can mean almost certain death, as the body cannot keep up with the strain of multiple drugs.

Heroin, alcohol, and benzodiazepines (tranquilizers) are all sedatives. They slow the nervous system and create a calming effect that delivers the typical feeling that heroin gives—a sense of having no problems in life. When these drugs are combined or taken in excess, the body slows down drastically. These functions slow down until they stop, which results in death. According to Dr. Sanjay Gupta, "As addicts take mixtures of drugs more chronically, they may not necessarily feel the effects of the narcotics, which still suppress the respiratory system. 'They're not feeling it, but it's still having an impact on their ability to breathe, and that's the real problem,' he said. 'It's called stacking. You can stack the same drug too close together, or you can start to stack other drugs, one on top of the other. That's how people get into trouble.'"[1]

The danger of drug mixing was brought into the spotlight with the death of two celebrated actors in the middle of the heroin epidemic. In July 2013, *Glee* actor Cory Monteith was found dead in his hotel room. The autopsy later revealed a combination of heroin and alcohol in his blood. In February 2014, Philip Seymour Hoffman of *The Hunger Games* was found dead with a syringe still in his arm. The autopsy concluded the actor died from a highly dangerous mixture of "heroin, cocaine, benzodiazepines and amphetamine."[2]

Heroin mixed with other drugs or alcohol is a highly lethal combination and was the cause of death of actor Cory Monteith.

1. Ray Sanchez, "Coroner: Philip Seymour Hoffman died of acute mixed drug intoxication," CNN, February 28, 2014. www.cnn.com/2014/02/28/showbiz/philip-seymour-hoffman-autopsy/.

2. Ray Sanchez, "Coroner: Philip Seymour Hoffman died of acute mixed drug intoxication."

Chapter Three

THE TRAP
OF ADDICTION

Heroin is a highly addictive drug, and it is estimated that 23 percent of people who try heroin become addicted and dependent on it. Heroin manipulates and changes the brain to the point that there is no such thing as the user waking up one day and saying they are going to quit using heroin. The path to recovery is often long, and the user goes through a battle to get to that point. It is a battle filled with painful withdrawal symptoms including a lack of interest in things that used to bring pleasure, such as getting together with friends. The painful withdrawal symptoms can kick in within hours after the last dose, and the user has to fight through instincts to use just to not go through withdrawal anymore.

How does a drug that was originally meant for pain relief trap so many in an addictive cycle? Part of it is due to prescription drugs—when someone becomes addicted to them, eventually, just like heroin, a tolerance builds, and that drug no longer offers any kind of relief. They then turn to heroin. Additionally, heroin offers a cheaper alternative for these users, but it leads them into another addictive cycle. What is more disturbing is that heroin is not perceived as a risky drug anymore. It is cheap, can be found easily, and as trends in the epidemic indicate, it is not going anywhere. Instead, it is trapping new users and causing more deaths each year.

To understand how someone becomes addicted and how to get out of the addiction cycle, it is necessary to understand the difference between addiction, tolerance, and dependence. Tolerance is when the body is becomes used to the dosage it has been receiving. The result is the heroin user then needs stronger heroin or a different way of taking heroin to feel the same as they used to while using it. For example, a heroin user who always inhaled heroin may switch to injecting heroin to get the strong initial rush that occurs immediately.

Dependence is when the user cannot function without heroin. The body does not function properly, and heroin becomes something the user needs just to feel like a normal, functioning person. However, this goes beyond just needing to feel normal. The brain and body change drastically with repetitive heroin use, and without heroin in the body, painful withdrawal symptoms present themselves.

Finally, addiction is when the user will go out of their way to get and use more heroin. The user may have had negative experiences such as overdoses. They may have come close to dying or experienced long-term effects such as pneumonia or infections. However, even though these problems have occurred, they are trapped and continue use because the positive experiences with the drug have imprinted on the brain so much that it is virtually impossible to see the damage it has actually caused.

Recognizing the Signs of Addiction

One day, a teenager is cheerful and communicative. The next, they are moody and defensive. They are secretive, exhibit odd behavior, and sometimes have fits of anger for no good reason. These are some of the possible warning signs of a substance abuse problem but—as any parent, teacher, or fellow student knows—they are often just a normal part of adolescent behavior.

For drug abusers, however, the drug habit begins to take a toll on their everyday lives. They lose interest in schoolwork and extracurricular activities. They may start hanging out with a new crowd of friends. They lie to hide their drug use and its consequences. Parents may be shocked to discover that their former model students are suddenly cutting class and stealing money from them. People addicted to heroin may steal money and valuables to support the addiction because they have used up all of their own money and resources to get the drug. Additionally, the user will seem secretive or lie to hide what is really going on. They may exhibit abnormal anxiety, depression, lethargy, aggressiveness, or other personality changes. Physical signs may include sudden weight loss, abnormal fatigue, or inattention to hygiene, and "track marks" from where heroin was injected may be present. In addition, there may be drug paraphernalia that the person would have no other reason to have, such as syringes without medical necessity.

Heroin is one of the most potent and addictive illegal drugs. Most teens recognize that it is too dangerous to experiment with, but some adolescents believe that they are immune to the risks. Teenagers are constantly looking for new experiences and ideas. They might believe that trying heroin once, just to see what it is like, will not hurt. They may think that adults exaggerate the potential dangers. Sometimes they are introduced to the drug by a friend or family member. In some cases, drug experimentation or other risky behaviors may be a symptom of underlying problems.

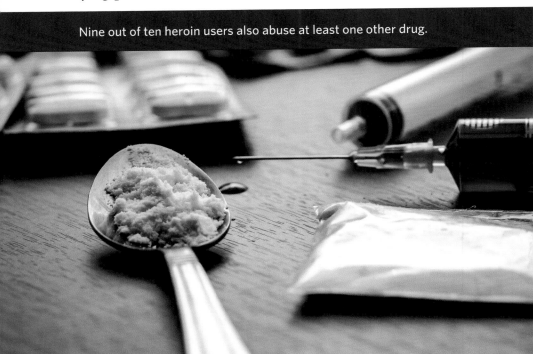

Nine out of ten heroin users also abuse at least one other drug.

Most new heroin users believe that they can control their use of the drug. They reason that if they use it only occasionally, they are in no danger of becoming addicted. Even after they become regular users, heroin abusers frequently remain in denial about the extent of their dependence on the drug.

Parents, friends, and teachers are often slow to recognize the warning signs of heroin abuse. They may have inaccurate preconceptions about the "typical" heroin user. Many people think that hard drugs are an inner city problem or that only the kids on the fringes of the social order at school would try heroin. In reality, heroin has spread to city suburbs and rural areas. The average age of users has fallen. Feature stories in newspapers may tell about the downfall of a star high school athlete or a promising young college graduate due to heroin. Old profiles of a "typical" heroin users are no longer accurate.

PRESCRIPTION PILL ABUSE

As of 2016, heroin and prescription painkillers were responsible for 30,000 deaths a year. Prescription painkillers are responsible for 80 percent of heroin addictions, while 45 percent of heroin users are still addicted to prescription painkillers even though they started using heroin. Once drugs such as OxyContin arrived on the market, doctors were prescribing painkillers much more freely for things such as back pain, and by 2000, doctors were writing about 6 million prescriptions a year for this particular drug. Overall, doctors wrote 76 million prescriptions for painkillers in 1991 and 219 million prescriptions in 2011. "Purdue Pharma, the creator of OxyContin, tried to reassure patients the drugs are rarely addictive,"[1] but statistics in recent years show how addictive these drugs really are. The rise in painkiller prescriptions was followed by the large heroin epidemic that is called the "worst drug crisis in American history."[2] How do so many turn from prescription painkillers to heroin? Eventually, these pills become expensive or start to have limited to no effect, and the user turns to the cheaper, yet more dangerous, relative of these pills: heroin.

Part of combatting the heroin epidemic is also dealing with the amount of prescription painkillers that are prescribed. However, these pills are often prescribed for people dealing with extraordinary amounts of pain, and they require them to function. Therefore, the elimination of them is impossible. As John Oliver reported, "There is not one simple answer here ... Not all opioid addicts will respond to the same treatments, and not all people in pain will find relief from alternative therapies. This is going to take a massive effort and a significant investment. It won't be cheap; it won't be quick; and it won't be easy."[3]

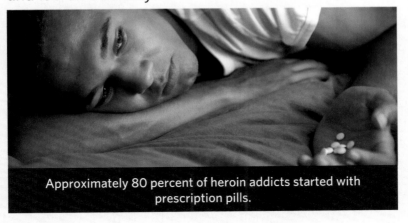

Approximately 80 percent of heroin addicts started with prescription pills.

1. Ryan Reed, "Watch John Oliver Rail on Big Pharma for Enabling Opioid Addiction," *Rolling Stone*, October 24, 2016. www.rolling-stone.com/tv/news/watch-john-oliver-rail-on-big-pharma-for-enabling-addiction-w446344.

2. Chris Amico and Dan Nolan, "Chasing Heroin: How Bad is the Opioid Epidemic?," PBS *Frontline*, February 23, 2016. www.pbs.org/wgbh/frontline/article/how-bad-is-the-opioid-epidemic/.

3. Ryan Reed, "Watch John Oliver Rail on Big Pharma for Enabling Opioid Addiction."

Destructive Consequences of Addiction

Heroin is notorious for the devastation it wreaks on an addict's health and life. For example, the practice of "backtracking," or withdrawing a small amount of blood into a syringe to ensure a good connection, contaminates the syringe with any diseases in the blood. Anybody else who uses the same syringe could be exposed to HIV, hepatitis, tuberculosis, or many other diseases.

"Cooking" heroin is generally not a sterile process either, and contaminants from the drug or the paraphernalia can irritate veins. If a drug user filters the liquefied drug with a piece of cotton cloth, they may get "cotton fever" from an immune reaction. A popular belief is that this reaction occurs when small bits of cotton accidentally get injected along with the heroin solution. However, cotton fever actually occurs due to bacteria that live in cotton plants. When cotton is prepared for consumer use in things such as cotton balls or swabs, a small amount of this bacteria still remains and is what causes cotton fever. Additionally, when the same syringe is used repeatedly, this bacteria can get trapped inside and create mold, which causes additional risks for addicts. Repeated injection in the same veins often leads to irritation, called phlebitis, and the user then must inject other sites. Fragments of undissolved heroin and other contaminants can cause permanent damage to blood vessels and other parts of the body.

Although mainlining is the most dangerous method of use, anyone who tries heroin will be exposed to additives used to "cut" heroin, or dilute its purity. There's no way of knowing the exact composition of a dose of heroin—it might contain sugar, talcum powder, quinine, other drugs such as caffeine or amphetamine, or even poisonous substances such as strychnine. The additives used to cut heroin can be toxic or, in some people, provoke an allergic reaction. They may cause respiratory illness if snorted.

As the heroin habit takes over an addict's life, he or she may begin to neglect hygiene, nutrition, and exercise. Addicts may lose weight, develop a weakened immune system, and take dangerous risks in order to satisfy their drug habit. Their desperation and impaired judgment can lead to disastrous results. Heroin addicts can alienate their friends and relatives, lose their jobs and homes, and face the legal repercussions of their actions. The broader consequences of heroin use affect families, communities, the legal system, and society in general.

TEN GREAT QUESTIONS TO ASK A COUNSELOR

Treating heroin addiction can be a long and difficult process, and it can make you feel isolated. Being educated and having a support system are essential, and talking with counselors either at school or in a treatment facility is important. Here is a list of 10 great questions to ask a counselor:

1. What resources are offered by my school or community for adolescents with substance abuse problems?

2. Some of my friends have told me that doing heroin once or twice is perfectly safe and that I should try it. What is the best way to let them know I am not interested?

3. I think that one of my friends is using heroin, but they will not admit that they have a problem. Who can I talk to about getting help for them?

4. My friends think that my drug use is out of control, but I do not think I have a problem. How can I tell if I am really addicted?

5. I am too ashamed to admit to my parents that I have a drug problem. How can I approach them?

6. I am recovering from a drug problem, and I feel like I do not fit in at school anymore. How can I get back into my old routine?

7. I am recovering from a drug problem, and I am constantly tempted to return to using heroin. How can I avoid relapsing?

8. I have used heroin in the past, and now I am experiencing health problems. Could these have been caused by drug use?

9. A friend of mine is recovering from a heroin problem. How can I help support them?

10. I hurt a lot of people's feelings when I had a drug problem, and now they do not trust me. How can I repair our relationships?

Addiction Science: Why It Is Hard to Quit

The damage that heroin does to the brain is evident in how hard it is for users to quit. Quitting heroin is not a simple decision such as deciding not to eat a donut or a whole bag of potato chips. As someone uses heroin, the receptors in the brain start to die off. Things that used to be enjoyable to the user are no longer enjoyable, and heroin becomes the only thing that is enjoyable to the user. Heroin is hard to quit due to this fact, but there are additional factors that make it so hard for heroin users to leave the habit behind for good.

Heroin seems to have such a positive effect on the brain—the initial rush of euphoria—that the brain creates a strong memory of this positive use. The side effects that last for hours after are overshadowed by the few minutes of happiness. Additionally, behavioral conditioning has a large role in heroin addiction. The brain becomes accustomed to the idea of enjoyable things:

> That's part of the reason it is so difficult for recovering addicts to stay clean over the long term. Sights, sounds and smells associated with the drug high—needles, for example, or the friends with whom they used to get high—prime this

dopamine response, and the motivation to seek the big reward of a drug hit builds. Recent research suggests that the connection between these cues and the motivation to seek a high strengthens over time in the brain of a hardened addict ... People who are addicted to drugs for years accumulate a large number of cues that lead them to seek out a high. Eventually, so much of their life becomes associated with getting high that it becomes nearly impossible for them to resist the urge.[28]

Once the heroin user becomes addicted to this degree, everything makes them think of using heroin, even things that do not seem related to the act of using it. Watching television, eating a meal, going to school or work, and getting together with friends become associated with using heroin. When the brain is in a normal, healthy state, healthy behaviors such as exercising or getting together with friends are rewarded in the brain. There is the surge of dopamine that makes the person feel good, and this becomes a motivator for continuing to do the action that was rewarded with the dopamine surge. Additionally, when there is fear or danger, a healthy brain makes a body react to stay out of danger. However, when someone is

addicted to a substance, that normal hardwiring of helpful brain processes can begin to work against you. Drugs ... hijack the pleasure/reward circuits in your brain and hook you into wanting more and more. Addiction can also send your emotional danger-sensing circuits into overdrive, making you feel anxious and stressed when you're not using the drugs ... At this stage, people often use drugs ... to keep from feeling bad rather than for their pleasurable effects. To add to that, repeated use of drugs can damage the essential decision-making center at the front of the brain. This area, known as the prefrontal cortex, is the very region that should help you recognize the harms of using addictive substances.[29]

Additionally, being a teenager makes these addiction factors even worse. Teenagers "are especially vulnerable to possible addiction because their brains are not yet fully developed—particularly the frontal regions that help with impulse control and assessing risk. Pleasure circuits in adolescent brains also operate in overdrive, making drug and alcohol use even more rewarding and enticing."[30] This is made even more troubling by the statistic that "20% of youths aged 12 to 17 reported that they saw either moderate, slight, or virtually no risk in using heroin."[31]

Long-term use of heroin creates a tolerance for and dependence on the deadly drug, which makes it extremely hard for addicts to simply quit.

ADDICTION: IS IT GENETIC?

One theory that scientists are testing is how much of addiction is genetic. Certain diseases such as cancer are known to run in families, and scientists have been studying twins to see if addiction can also run in families, and to what degree.

Twins are ideal for research due to the similarity in DNA; however, there is a larger factor that makes them ideal candidates—they are generally exposed to the same environmental stresses. In these twin studies, scientists study both identical and fraternal twins and compare the results. If addiction is genetic, then each twin in the identical pair would be addicted to drugs or not addicted to drugs. The fraternal twins, on the other hand, have DNA that is like that of non-twin brothers or sisters. In other words, it is not as similar as that of identical twins because fraternal twins have a gene similarity of 50 percent, just like non-twin siblings, whereas identical twins have a 100 percent gene similarity. With studying fraternal twins, there were more variations in the results—one twin would be addicted to drugs while the other was not.

The researchers found that there is a 50 percent chance of addiction being genetic—when one twin was addicted, the other twin had a 50/50 chance of also being addicted. However, while there is a 50 percent chance of being addicted to drugs when another family member is addicted, genes are not the only factor. Just because a sibling has a drug addiction, it does not mean that another sibling automatically will as well. Similarly, "not all members of an affected family are necessarily prone to addiction."[1]

1. "Biology of Addiction: Drugs and Alcohol Can Hijack Your Brain," *NIH News in Health*, October 2015. newsinhealth.nih.gov/issue/oct2015/feature1.

Breaking Addiction: Seeking Treatment

When someone who is addicted to heroin is seeking treatment, having the support of family and friends is essential. Heroin's reputation used to be that of a drug that was only used in impoverished areas. However, the recent epidemic has affected people from all walks of life, including the wealthy. The past stereotypes of heroin users created a stigma that can make a user feel isolated, and having the support of loved ones is essential in getting clean. Some heroin addicts recognize their drug problem before it can take a toll on their lives. Others refuse to admit their addiction until they hit bottom, triggered by an event such as expulsion from school, an overdose, or an accident. Some users require an intervention, in which family or friends formally express their concern and urge the user to get help.

Quitting heroin not only involves painful withdrawal symptoms and possible relapse, but also a complete change of habits and way of thinking to get the brain back into a normal pattern of thinking. There are a variety of treatment options offered to those addicted to heroin, and treatment generally starts with detoxification, which is ridding the body of the drug. When the user abruptly quits using heroin, withdrawal symptoms occur. Withdrawal can be highly uncomfortable, but it is not deadly. The greatest danger that occurs during the withdrawal phase is using heroin again to avoid the discomfort. The most successful instances of detoxification take place in a facility rather than alone to ensure that the user does not go back to heroin, and also, a facility gradually detoxes the user to ease some of the discomfort rather than taking all of the drug away all at once.

There are two primary approaches to treating heroin addiction. One method is to replace heroin with another opiate that is less potent and dangerous. The most common substitute is the opioid methadone, which shares some common effects with heroin. Methadone staves off withdrawal and the craving for heroin but does not itself give the "high" of heroin. It also blocks the euphoric properties of heroin, so the two drugs cannot be used in combination. An addict may stay on methadone indefinitely, which is called methadone maintenance. The second method is when the facility weans the user off the drug by giving gradually smaller doses. The body becomes used to the drug level until eventually the user is given none.

Heroin addiction is very difficult to break. For this reason, the best course for a recovering addict is to enter a drug treatment program run by experienced professionals. Rehabilitation options include inpatient programs, outpatient programs, and therapeutic communities. Inpatient treatment programs involve the former user staying at a sober living facility. They are separated from external stresses and are allowed to solely focus on recovery. Outpatient treatment programs allow the former user to live at home while attending treatments and counseling at a facility. Drug abusers enrolled in outpatient programs attend group counseling and therapy daily or a few times a week, depending on the intensity of the program. Therapeutic communities and methadone treatment have been found to benefit teenagers the most: "Living in a sober community free of triggers to use may strengthen adolescents' ability to remain abstinent. Medication therapy may be especially helpful in reducing cravings and external temptations as they cope with bodily changes and teen-specific social struggles," which include "self-esteem and peer influence."[32]

Throughout the rehabilitation process, there is a large focus on the psychological and behavioral aspects of what made the person use heroin in the first place. The user works "with medical personnel to uncover what [their] reasons are for using and to learn how to heal from past hurts and find new ways to cope with them in the future."[33] While the detox process can last about seven days, the therapy and treatment portion is what is most important to the individual's success in staying drug-free, and this part of the process tends to last much longer. The length of the time in therapy and treatment depend on the individual's needs, with some structured treatments lasting anywhere from 6 to 12 months. It does not help that the transition back into normal life can be difficult. Individuals will have to face new problems caused by their addictions. They may have to fix relationships, resolve legal situations, deal with financial issues, and regain their health.

However, some rehabilitation centers have wait lists to get into treatment. With the number of users sharply increasing during the recent heroin epidemic, rehabilitation centers are filling up, which leaves many heroin users who desire to come clean feeling helpless and frustrated. "In Massachusetts, substance abusers have to wait weeks to get help. In Florida, it's a month. Wait times are as long as 18 months in Maine." One woman in Ohio was so desperate to get clean that she asked a judge to send her to jail. She said, "There's no help out there anymore ... There's a three-month waiting list for any rehab around here because of the heroin epidemic." Another man in Maine also used jail as a way to get clean from heroin and said, "The jails here are basically detox facilities."[34] In Snohomish County, Washington, the jails have essentially been detox centers since 2013. However, jail is not a substitute for a rehabilitation center. The user may

A heroin addiction can make a person feel extremely alone, so a support system, including family, friends, and counselors, is essential in overcoming addiction.

get clean, but they do not have the resources needed to stay clean in the long-term. The heroin epidemic created a new crisis: a population of heroin users who want to get clean but cannot get the resources and help needed to do so.

Withdrawal and Relapse: The Tough Road to Recovery

The human body quickly adapts to functioning with the constant presence of heroin, and when the effects of a dose of heroin wear off, the body must readjust to its absence. This is the reason for the physical signs of withdrawal. Many withdrawal symptoms are the opposite of heroin's initial effects on a first-time user. A new heroin user feels euphoria, warmth, and relief from pain, for example. Heroin use also causes constipation. A user going through withdrawal, by contrast, will experience restlessness and acute anxiety, chills, hypersensitivity to pain, and diarrhea.

The onset of withdrawal is marked by flu-like symptoms such as a runny nose, sweating, and changes in body temperature. Further signs include muscle cramps and pains, irritability, and headaches. Withdrawal also often causes insomnia, which worsens addicts' ability to cope with the psychological effects of withdrawal. While recovering from using heroin,

the body adapts to chronic overstimulation of opioid receptors by increasing the number of them on the surface of brain cells, so that more receptors need to be activated by opioid drugs to produce an effect. Also, the amount of endorphins, the natural chemicals that activate opiate receptors, is decreased in chronic opioid drug users as the body compensates for overstimulation of this system. These adaptations have been linked to increased pain sensitivity and mood disturbances in individuals addicted to opiates. These changes can take months or even years to completely reverse themselves and for opiate signaling to return to normal levels.[34]

The path to recovery from drug addiction is not easy, and the relapse rate for former heroin addicts is very high. Upon returning to school, a teenager might start hanging out with the same crowd again and may return to using drugs as well. A

Today's Heroin Epidemic: Demanding a Different Approach

It was previously believed that heroin was a drug that was used in impoverished neighborhoods and particularly used among the homeless. During President Richard Nixon's war on drugs that focused on cocaine and "poor, predominantly black urban areas, the public response was defined by zero tolerance and stiff prison sentences."[1] However, with the recent epidemic, the demographic of users and the conversation changed. An increasing number of heroin users are from the "middle-class or wealthy," and "nearly 90 percent of the people who tried heroin for the first time in the past decade were white."[2] As such, the public no longer demanded zero tolerance and prison sentences for drug crimes.

As the epidemic hit suburbs and many families lost children and siblings due to heroin, these same families wanted language altered. Instead of a crime, families wanted it treated as a disease. Instead of a prison sentence, families wanted it treated with rehabilitation. The families' anger and demands did not go unheard. During his presidency, Barack Obama revealed a $133 million plan to tackle the heroin epidemic. The plan started with training for health care providers on prescribing painkillers—where 80 percent of heroin addictions start—and also included additional treatment programs for heroin users to get help. In addition, some law enforcement agencies started unconventional programs that allowed users to turn in their needles without a drug charge occurring as a result.

1. Katharine Q. Seelye, "In Heroin Crisis, White Families Seek Gentler War on Drugs," *New York Times*, October 30, 2015. www.nytimes.com/2015/10/31/us/heroin-war-on-drugs-parents.html?_r=1.

2. Katharine Q. Seelye, "The Numbers Behind America's Heroin Epidemic," *New York Times*, October 30, 2015. www.nytimes.com/interactive/2015/10/30/us/31heroin-deaths.html?_r=0.

former addict may be unable to cope with depression, anxiety, and other psychological troubles that might linger long after physical withdrawal has passed. The teen might think that using the drug just one time, perhaps at a party, will not bring about a return to addiction.

Withdrawal from heroin involves things such as drug cravings, anxiety, and depression. These can last anywhere from a few months to years.

Recovering users often have trouble staying away from heroin unless they completely change their lifestyle. Addicts tend to react to certain triggers related to drug use—smokers might habitually light a cigarette after a meal or reach for one during a stressful situation. In the same way, the sight of drug

paraphernalia or a visit from a former drug buddy might cause cravings for heroin. A recovering addict has a better chance of avoiding relapse if they can avoid reminders of heroin use.

Medication Implants: The Future of Combatting the Epidemic

The increasing use of heroin and heroin-related deaths has doctors and officials looking for new ways to treat heroin dependence and end the epidemic. In May 2016, the Food and Drug Administration (FDA) approved a new way of treating heroin dependence—a medication implant.

The implant involves four tiny, 1-inch (2.54 cm) rods inserted under the skin in the upper arm. Each rod contains the medication Probuphine, which is made from the semisynthetic opioid buprenorphine. The implants last six months and provide a "constant, low-level dose of buprenorphine."[35] The implants are

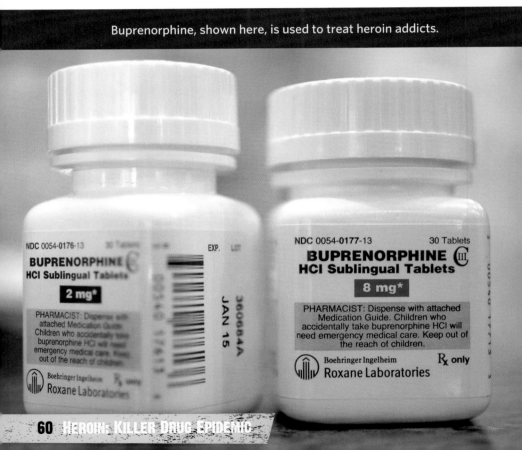

Buprenorphine, shown here, is used to treat heroin addicts.

revolutionary in treating dependence, but they are not meant for heroin users that are just starting recovery. The Probuphine implant is to be used "in patients who are already stable on low-to-moderate doses of other forms of buprenorphine, as part of a complete treatment program."[36] The medication implants allow former heroin users in recovery the chance to lead a normal life without remembering to take medication daily.

The other positive side of the medication implants is that the former user cannot purposely forget to take their medication in order to have an excuse to use heroin again. The recovering user also cannot sell it illegally, which they may do with the pills. In addition, the implants prevent the abuse of medication. Finally, the implants eliminate the possibility of pills becoming lost and throwing off the individual's treatment plan, which can result in a relapse.

Chapter Four

THE LEGALITY OF HEROIN

Heroin has a long, complicated history of being first legal then illegal. Since the invention of heroin from morphine, officials have struggled with combatting addiction to the drug. From mere restrictions on heroin in the early 1900s to the war on drugs and the current epidemic, heroin has not gone anywhere, even with restrictions and laws. In fact, it has only become more widespread, with devastating results.

The changing field of heroin use and the rising numbers in both heroin use and heroin-related deaths have authorities scrambling to end the epidemic and save lives. This changing field has also brought about a change in the conversation surrounding drug abuse and addiction. As the epidemic continued to take thousands of lives, the conversation turned to thinking of users as having a disorder and a demand for a person-centered approach.

A Legal History of Heroin

In 1914, the passage of the Harrison Narcotics Act by Congress became the first measure intended to regulate drug use in the United States. The new law placed stiffer regulations on derivatives of coca (the source of cocaine) and opium. Both drugs were still legal, but now, there were new taxes and restrictions that applied to their sale. Overall, the Harrison Act failed to curb drug use. Instead, it caused many morphine and codeine addicts to switch to heroin, which was cheaper and more potent, and it drove addicts to the black market.

In 1924, heroin was finally made illegal with the Heroin Act. This act made possession of heroin and manufacturing of heroin illegal, which in turn, forced addicts to purchase the drug illegally on the streets. Even with the passage of the Heroin Act, there were still problems with heroin, and in 1956, the Narcotics Control Act stiffened penalties for drug offenses. In 1970, the Controlled Substance Act overhauled and consolidated all previous drug laws. The principles behind this law are still in place today.

In 1971, President Richard Nixon declared a war on drugs, and he oversaw the creation of the DEA in 1973. In the 1980s, as abuse of crack cocaine began to spread in the United States, President Ronald Reagan announced yet another war on drugs, and First Lady Nancy Reagan announced the "Just Say No" campaign. The campaign, quite simply, told people that when confronted with drugs, to "Just Say No." Although Reagan's war on drugs concentrated on reducing the supply by fighting the international drug trade, new laws passed during the 1980s dramatically increased the number of offenders imprisoned for drug possession.

In 2000, the Drug Addiction Treatment Act allowed physicians to prescribe narcotics to treat opioid dependency. However, each physician's office could only treat 30 patients, even if there were multiple physicians in the office. In 2005, President George W. Bush amended the Controlled Substances Act to eliminate this limit of 30 patients per office, and by 2006, offices were allowed to treat 100 patients at a time. This limit was increased again in 2016 to 275 patients. Also in 2016, the Comprehensive Addiction and Recovery Act again amended the Controlled Substances Act, and under it, nurses and physician assistants could prescribe buprenorphine for opioid dependence.

Heroin Smuggling

Even though heroin has been illegal since the early 1920s, it is still widespread and still makes its way into countries such as the United States through complicated systems. It seems technological and transportation advances are to blame:

In other words, globalization has led to an explosion of drug trafficking. More than 420 million shipping containers traverse the seas every year, transporting 90 percent of the world's cargo. Most carry legitimate goods, but authorities cannot inspect them all, and some are used to smuggle drugs— or just as importantly, the chemicals used to make meth and cheaply process coca leaves and opium poppies into cocaine and heroin. Airplanes, submarines, speedboats, trucks, tunnels— taken as a whole, the systems used to move illegal drugs around the world comprise a logistics network likely bigger than Amazon, FedEx, and UPS combined.[37]

How illegal drugs move around the world constantly changes. As soon as authorities find out routes and laws change, the routes change as well. A number of countries add to the world's heroin supply—Myanmar, Thailand, and Laos included. However, there is one country that provides nearly all of the world's heroin and worries the United States the most: Afghanistan.

Heroin is smuggled into the United States from countries such as Afghanistan, Colombia, and Mexico.

Afghanistan produces 95 percent of all heroin and opiates in the world.

Mexico has also created a heroin problem for the United States due its close proximity. Every car is inspected while crossing the border between Mexico and the United States, and each part of the car is checked. Smugglers may go to any length to get heroin from Mexico into the United States, and they use sophisticated systems to do so, including hiding packages of heroin in gas tanks or a crate of soda bottles that looks like a regular shipment of the beverage. A large amount of heroin that makes its way from Mexico into the United States is smuggled in cars or taken to houses in cities near the border such as San Diego and Los Angeles that are specifically reserved for the purpose of stashing heroin. If the smuggler makes it across the border, the heroin they were carrying can make it across the United States within three days, and this further fuels the epidemic.

Legal Consequences

The Controlled Substances Act of 1970 categorized drugs by five "schedules," according to their potential for abuse. Schedule I drugs are the most tightly controlled, with a high potential for abuse and no accepted medical use. Schedule V drugs, which are not tightly controlled, have legitimate medical uses and do not require a prescription from a doctor. Heroin and many other potent opiates and opioids are classified as Schedule I controlled substances.

What is the penalty for possessing heroin? It must be understood that "possession" of a drug in a legal sense means having the drug in your control, not necessarily on your body or with your belongings. If the drug is in a room that you share with others, for example, the police may conclude that you are in possession of it.

Laws concerning illegal drugs are difficult to navigate. They vary depending on whether federal or state jurisdiction applies, and they vary from one state to anotther. Drug laws are also amended frequently. Federal laws and some state laws have sentencing guidelines, while other laws allow the prosecutor and other officials involved in the case to consider extenuating factors.

Depending on the offense, a drug crime can be considered a misdemeanor or a felony. A misdemeanor is a minor crime punishable by community service or a short jail sentence. A felony is a serious crime punishable by a harsh sentence. Possession of between 100 grams and 999 grams of heroin carries a federal sentence of at least 5 years in prison if it is the first offense. If it is the second offense, it carries a prison sentence of at least 10 years. Possession of 1 kilogram or more carries a minimum 10-year sentence if it is the first offense, whereas the second offense carries a minimum 20-year sentence. If there are prior offenses for heroin possession, the prison sentence is life.

Certain factors are likely to increase penalties. Individuals can be prosecuted for "conspiracy" with a drug offender even if they did not commit a crime—for instance, letting the drug offender borrow a car could be interpreted as aiding a drug offense. Prosecutors may push for an "intent to distribute" conviction—punishable by a tougher sentence than possession—even if the offender claims a drug stash was for his or her own use. Adults get

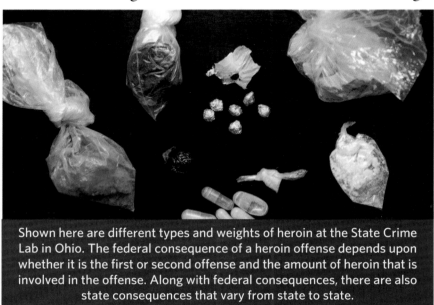

Shown here are different types and weights of heroin at the State Crime Lab in Ohio. The federal consequence of a heroin offense depends upon whether it is the first or second offense and the amount of heroin that is involved in the offense. Along with federal consequences, there are also state consequences that vary from state to state.

FROM POPPY FIELDS IN AFGHANISTAN TO THE SUBURBS

A few countries grow heroin and supply it into different parts of the world, but Afghanistan dominates the market by providing nearly all of the world's heroin supply. Afghanistan is the world's top grower of opium poppies, producing over 95 percent of all opiates.

For the United States, the opium situation in Afghanistan goes beyond the issue of drug production. A coalition led by the United States invaded Afghanistan in 2001 to combat terrorism and install a democratic government. The U.S. invasion of Afghanistan coincided with a surge in poppies and heroin production in Afghanistan. In 2001, Afghan poppy farmers grew about 20,000 acres (8,000 ha) of poppies. In 2014, that number increased to 535,500 acres (224,000 ha). Additionally, Afghanistan produces about 375 tons of heroin each year, compared with 26 tons in Mexico and 50 tons in Myanmar. This large amount of heroin then makes its way around the world through complicated cargo and shipping systems.

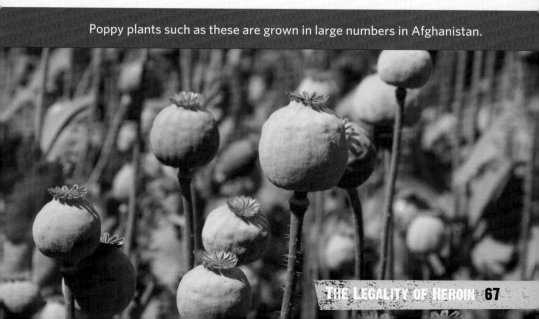

Poppy plants such as these are grown in large numbers in Afghanistan.

particularly stiff sentences for committing a drug offense within a school zone and for supplying minors with drugs.

Drug Policy

Is the United States winning the war on drugs? Supporters of current antidrug policies point out that sting operations by the DEA have disrupted Mexican and Colombian drug cartels and intercepted tons of heroin destined for the United States. They believe that strict sentencing for drug offenders is justified and that it acts as a deterrent for would-be drug users.

Reform advocates counter that efforts to curb drug trafficking have not reduced the flow of heroin into the United States. They claim that strict sentencing has packed prisons with nonviolent minor drug offenders at taxpayer expense.

It is unlikely that there will be any significant trend toward loosening the drug laws in the near future. No lawmaker wants to be viewed as "soft on drugs." When former President Bill Clinton took office in 1993, it was predicted that he would have a more lenient stance on drugs than the presidents before him. Instead, Clinton poured money into antidrug programs during his presidency, and in 1996, he appointed retired four-star military general Barry McCaffrey to serve as "drug czar" and coordinate antidrug efforts.

Drug policy is a hotly debated issue:

Depending upon whom you ask, we are currently either doing too much in terms of prosecuting drug addicts and other offenders, or not enough. It is hard to dispute that the criminalization has done anything except lead to the overcrowding of our prisons ... One area where we have not focused enough energy is the rehabilitation of drug addicts. Some say we have been too preoccupied with putting drug users in prison as opposed to helping them get the help they need via drug rehab.[38]

The drug policy has started to see some change with marijuana being approved for medicinal use in some states and completely legalized in others. However, marijuana is still categorized as a Schedule I drug—just like heroin—which means it has "no currently accepted medical use and a high potential for abuse."[39] Additionally, although marijuana is legalized in some states and approved for medicinal use in others, it is still illegal at the federal level. There is virtually no chance that heroin will ever be widely legalized. However, some individuals have called for reform of the current drug policy in the middle of the largest heroin epidemic the United States has seen, because "after 40 years and a trillion dollars, the nation has little to show for its war on drugs. Prisons are beyond crowded and there's a new outbreak in the heroin epidemic."[40]

Director ("drug czar") of the National Drug Control Policy, Michael Botticelli, is even calling for reform of the drug policy. His belief is that "addicts should be patients, not prisoners,"[41] and that addiction cannot be taken out of people by arresting them and putting them in jail. His approach is focused on rehabilitation but not legalization of drugs such as heroin or marijuana. Instead, his focus is to turn the drug policy into more of a person-centered approach. Additionally, his goal is to shift the vocabulary and change the conversation around addiction by replacing it with the word "disorder" to remove the stigma attached to substance abuse.

Laced Heroin: A New Lethal Drug

The recent heroin epidemic has taken the lives of thousands of people each year. Although heroin on its own is highly addictive and an overdose can quickly mean death, the epidemic also saw the rise of an even deadlier version of heroin, and that is heroin laced with other drugs such as fentanyl or Carfentanil.

These deadly batches of heroin affected not only families, but entire communities. In Erie County, New York, there were 200 overdoses each month in 2015, and the area was hit hard by heroin laced with fentanyl. In 2016, there was an average of 10 deaths per week, with 30 more deaths between January and April of 2016 than in the same time period of 2015.

This is not the first time fentanyl-laced heroin created a public health threat. In 2006, there was an outbreak of fentanyl-laced heroin. This mixture was believed to be responsible for 14 deaths between May and July in one community, with doctors saying that it seemed to die down. However, the fentanyl-laced heroin epidemic did not die down. Instead, it became the focus of a much larger epidemic years later.

In August 2016, in just one week in Ohio, there were about 96 heroin overdoses that resulted in death. The drug that was to blame was heroin laced with Carfentanil. This drug adds power to the feeling heroin delivers, but it "is the most potent commercial opioid in the world … It is 10,000 times stronger than morphine, and at least 100 times more powerful than its analog, the opioid fentanyl."[42] The power of this drug is shown in its accepted use: to sedate zoo animals such as elephants. "It takes just two milligrams of Carfentanil to knock out a 2,000-pound African elephant, and the veterinarians who administer the drug use gloves and face masks to prevent exposure to it, because a dose the size of a grain of salt could kill a person—and may be lethal even when absorbed through the skin."[43] Additionally, naloxone, the medication that can turn around an overdose, barely has an effect on turning around an overdose when Carfentanil is involved.

A new drug to make its way into communities and take lives with it is the synthetic heroin substitute called Pink, or U-47700 as it is known to chemists. Pink is "eight times stronger than heroin," and "is so powerful that if you touch it, you could go into cardiac arrest."[44] Additionally, this new drug is not yet illegal in all states. When new drugs arrive on the scene, authorities find it hard to keep up in making them illegal, and while this happens, more lives are lost. In the first 9 months of 2016, about 80 deaths across the United States were caused by the new deadly heroin substitute Pink.

Fentanyl and Carfentanil are virtually undetectable in heroin. When the user purchases an amount of heroin, they do not know what is in it. It could even not be heroin, or it could be more like another drug that is laced with heroin instead of just being heroin or heroin laced with a tiny amount of another drug. A safe injection facility in Vancouver, Canada, ran a trial on testing the composition of heroin that users brought into their facility so users could know exactly what was in it. The results were startling—86 percent of the heroin brought in was laced with fentanyl, the drug behind thousands of deaths.

Heroin laced with other substances, such as fentanyl, creates a deadly concoction that is the cause of many heroin-related deaths.

DANGER
contains **Fentanyl**
(Highly toxic, May be fatal)

w sirchie.c n

SIRCHIE Products • Vehicles •

NALOXONE

Naloxone is an opiate antagonist that can mean life for someone who suffered a heroin overdose. The medication can be given to the individual by injection or through a nasal spray to counter the overdose. Naloxone "binds to opioid receptors and can reverse and block the effects of other opioids. It can very quickly restore normal respiration to a person whose breathing has slowed or stopped as a result of overdosing with heroin or prescription opioid pain medications."[1]

Naloxone has the ability to stop an overdose immediately after it is administered, if it is administered in time. However, while it has the ability to save someone's life who has overdosed, it is not a cure. The user will still experience cravings for heroin, and even though an overdose has been experienced, it often is not enough to inspire them to get help, or finding help after the traumatic event can be difficult. After naloxone is administered, the individual needs follow-up care to make a change in their lifestyle: "Lying in the emergency room after being revived, many addicts say they experience a fleeting moment of clarity that makes them receptive to help. But that potential is often lost in a patchwork healthcare system that gives survivors little incentive to change. Many walk out of the hospital with just a list of treatment options on their discharge papers."[2] Heroin changes the brain's chemistry, and knowledge of the danger of the act of using heroin is overshadowed by the few minutes of euphoria, a fact that police and medical personnel are witnessing as they treat the same people for heroin overdoses multiple times.

Naloxone can often mean life or death for an overdose victim.

1, "Naloxone," National Institute on Drug Abuse, September 2016. www.drugabuse.gov/related-topics/naloxone.

2. Jon Schuppe, "Beyond Narcan: Why Heroin Addicts Need More Than an Overdose Antidote," NBC News, December 23, 2014. www.nbcnews.com/storyline/americas-heroin-epidemic/beyond-narcan-why-heroin-addicts-need-more-overdose-antidote-n269351.

Chapter Five

TACKLING THE EPIDEMIC

The recent heroin epidemic has taken thousands of lives each year and left families wanting answers and calling for reforms. Most importantly, they have wanted programs to help addicts. Use has skyrocketed among new demographics such as the middle class and wealthy, and the epidemic has turned into a public health threat. Now, heroin kills more people than car accidents. Between 2010 and 2014, there was a 267 percent rise in deaths from heroin for white people, while black people had a 213 percent rise, Latinos had a 137 percent increase, and Native Americans had a 236 percent increase.

How did heroin become so prevalent? In part, it is due to the mass prescribing of prescription pain pills. They are expensive, and after a certain amount of time, it is not enough. In contrast, heroin is readily available and much cheaper with a greater effect—the cost can be as little as $4, which initially seems appealing for many people, not just those in pain.

The Deadly Rise in Heroin Use

On June 6, 2006, 17-year-old Joseph Krecker was found slumped over in his Jeep Cherokee on Chicago's West Side. The cause of his death was easily determined: Krecker was still clutching a bag of heroin.

Krecker's death occurred among a string of heroin-related fatalities and nonlethal overdoses. The cause of this 2006 outbreak was a concoction of potent heroin mixed with fentanyl. The drug combination quickly earned the nickname "Get High or Die Trying." Authorities warned the public about the dangers of the mixture, but the strategy backfired. Addicts swarmed the

THE PUBLIC HEALTH THREAT OF HEROIN

According to the Centers for Disease Control (CDC), "Public health is the science of protecting and improving the health of families and communities through promotion of healthy lifestyles, research for disease and injury prevention and detection and control of infectious diseases."[1] The rise in heroin abuse and death has created a serious public health issue, and a large part of it stems from prescription pills. People become addicted to these pills and then eventually turn to heroin. In fact, some states have more prescriptions given than there are people living in the state. The solution, some feel, starts with doctors cutting back on prescriptions and finding alternatives to treating pain. However, education also goes a long way in this, with patients being educated about the overall effects of the drug that is prescribed. Additionally, others feel that the way to fix the safety issue of heroin overdoses is for addicts themselves to be educated on what heroin does and how to treat an overdose. The overall theme in ending the public health threat and epidemic according to families and some authorities is this: Remove the stigma that is attached to heroin use, treat it as a disorder, and offer help instead of punishment. The public health threat of heroin also goes beyond just using heroin—it also spreads diseases such as HIV and hepatitis, which affect those who do not even use heroin. Heroin has become a "full-blown health crisis that cuts across geographic, social, racial and economic boundaries."[2]

1. "What is Public Health?," CDC Foundation. www.cdcfoundation.org/content/what-public-health.

2. James Pilcher and Lisa Bernard-Kuhn, "Chasing the heroin resurgence," *USA Today*. www.usatoday.com/story/news/nation-now/2014/06/12/communities-across-usa-scramble-to-tackle-heroin-surge/9713463/.

areas where they thought they might obtain the fentanyl-laced heroin, and the death count continued to rise.

More than a century after heroin was first made, it is still destroying lives and causing heartbreak. It has survived numerous attempts to stem its availability and abuse. As the outbreak of heroin-fentanyl deaths demonstrates, drug trends evolve over time. There are many resources that alleviate some aspects of the heroin problem—education, prevention, harm-reduction programs, drug treatment, and incarceration—but after a century of debate, the only point of agreement on all sides of the issue is that with heroin, there is no easy solution.

The heroin epidemic has not discriminated based on race, and it has affected all ages. In 2014, per 100,000 people age 15 to 24, 3.3 died due to heroin overdose. What is even more disturbing is at what age heroin use starts. In surveys taken from 2007 to 2012, when asked if they had used heroin within the past month, 150,000 12-year-olds said they had. In 2012, that number increased to nearly 350,000.

Not only are the figures drastically increasing, but the desperation of heroin addicts is, as well. Heroin is thought of as something a user does in a private residence. However, during this recent epidemic, heroin users have been injecting heroin in the public eye:

> *A man riding a city bus at rush hour injected heroin into his hand, in full view of other passengers ... several people overdosed in the bathrooms of a historic church ... With heroin cheap and widely available on city streets throughout the country, users are making their buys and shooting up as soon as they can, often in public places. Police officers are routinely finding drug users—unconscious or dead—in cars, in the bathrooms of fast-food restaurants, on mass transit and in parks, hospitals and libraries.*[45]

The need for heroin is such that physically and mentally, the user has to take it the first chance they get, which is often in the view of the public. The fact that the addict needs to use in front of the public where they could be caught and arrested highlights

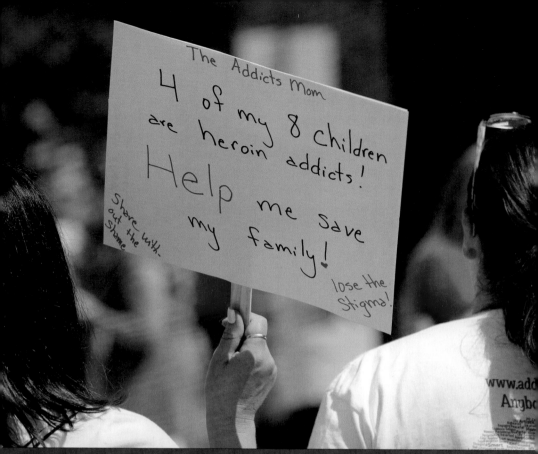

The Addicts mom

4 of my 8 children are heroin addicts! Help me save my family!

Share out the Shame with.

lose the Stigma!

www.add
Amybc

Heroin use among 18- to 25-year-olds has increased more than 109 percent and has affected numerous families.

how the current drug policy and war on drugs are not, in the end, effective.

In fact, "drug overdoses are driving up the death rate of young white adults in the United States to levels not seen since the end of the AIDS epidemic more than two decades ago ... In 2014, the overdose death rate for whites ages 25 to 34 was five times its level in 1999, and the rate for 35- to 44-year-old whites tripled during that period"[46] However, black people have largely been spared in the heroin epidemic. This is due to the fact that heroin addiction often starts with prescription pill addiction, and a racist stereotype is actually protecting this demographic: "Doctors are much more reluctant to prescribe painkillers to minority patients, worrying that they might sell them or become addicted."[47]

How to End the Epidemic

Ending the heroin epidemic is not something that will happen overnight, nor is it something that can be ended with just one approach. The epidemic has reached unprecedented levels in both death rates and use rates, and ending it requires many people from different levels of authority.

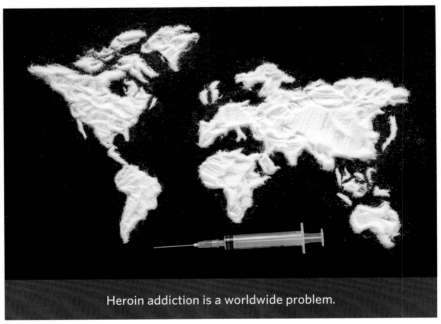

Heroin addiction is a worldwide problem.

HEROIN EPIDEMIC AWARENESS WEEK

In September 2016, President Barack Obama instituted the first Prescription Opioid and Heroin Epidemic Awareness Week, stating,

Each year, more Americans die from drug overdoses than in traffic accidents, and more than three out of five of these deaths involve an opioid. Since 1999, the number of overdose deaths involving opioids, including prescription opioid pain relievers, heroin, and fentanyl, *has nearly quadrupled. Many people who die from an overdose struggle with an opioid use disorder or other substance use disorder, and unfortunately misconceptions surrounding these disorders have contributed to harmful stigmas that prevent individuals from seeking evidence-based treatment ... I continue to call on the Congress to provide $1.1 billion to expand access to treatment services for opioid use disorder ... We are also working to improve opioid prescribing practices and support targeted enforcement activities ... because the longer we go without congressional action on this funding, the more opportunities we miss to save lives.[1]*

In 2016, President Barack Obama announced the first Prescription Opioid and Heroin Epidemic Awareness Week.

1. Barack Obama, "Presidential Proclamation – Prescription Opioid and Heroin Epidemic Awareness Week, 2016," The White House, September 16, 2016. www.whitehouse.gov/the-press-office/2016/09/16/presidential-proclamation-prescription-opioid-and-heroin-epidemic.

To start, President Barack Obama directed important steps that were aimed at prescription drugs, with the knowledge that this is how a large amount of heroin addictions begin. The first step is prescriber training: Anyone who prescribes opioids must be trained on prescribing them as well as their effects and risks. Second, "Federal Departments and Agencies that directly provide, contract to provide, reimburse for, or otherwise facilitate access to health benefits [must] conduct a review to identify barriers to medication-assisted treatment for opioid use disorders and develop action plans to address these barriers."[48] The CDC adopted these points into their list for how to end the epidemic on a state level, also including the following:

- *Expand access to and training for administering naloxone to reduce opioid overdose deaths.*

- *Ensure that people have access to integrated prevention services, including access to sterile injection equipment from a reliable source, as allowed by local policy.*

- *Help local jurisdictions to put these effective practices to work in communities where drug addiction is common.*[49]

Next, as National Drug Control Policy director Michael Botticelli stated, the stigma of addiction must be removed in order for users to get the help that is needed. Removing the stigma and treating use more as a disorder than an addiction may make users more open to seeking help, thus reducing the use and death rates in the United States.

Although naloxone is proving to be useful in turning around an overdose, it is not a cure or treatment. It is temporary, and should be treated as such. Heroin users need more than just an antidote, especially when these users are teenagers. Given the scope of the epidemic and the fact that it is not slowing down and only getting worse, some have unconventional ideas on how to best help users and end the epidemic in the process.

Methadone substitution and other treatment programs can enable former heroin addicts to make changes in their lives, but some critics claim that methadone treatment merely exchanges

This quilt was made in memory of people who have died in the opioid and heroin epidemic.

one addiction for another. Even proponents have mixed feelings. Drug treatment organizations often receive complaints from neighbors when they propose opening a new methadone clinic. Residents may say that although they respect the work the organization is doing, they do not want drug addicts hanging around near their homes.

Some other programs intended to help drug addicts are even more controversial. These "harm-reduction" programs focus on reducing the likelihood of overdose and other risks associated with heroin use. One tactic is offering syringe and needle exchanges, in which an addict can confidentially trade used syringes and needles for sterile ones. Needle-exchange programs have been shown to reduce the transmission of HIV and other diseases among drug users. Harm-reduction programs also educate participants on minimizing risk when using heroin and may teach how to recognize and respond to an overdose. Some states and communities operate harm-reduction programs, although the federal government does not. Opponents of harm-reduction programs allege that such measures condone drug use and that addicts should instead be punished for illegal drug activity.

The most controversial treatment for heroin addiction and dependence is heroin-assisted treatment. The treatment is controversial because it goes against the way that people think about getting clean from heroin use—the treatment actually gives the addict heroin.

Switzerland developed a trial on prescribing heroin to heroin addicts as part of a treatment program. The individual would be given daily injections as part of their treatment plan. It worked so well that Switzerland incorporated it into their laws with supervised injection facilities. The treatment is meant to help heroin addicts get their lives back together and either slowly wean them off of the drug or provide a maintenance dose, and it does so in a nonjudgmental setting. The people-centered approach has worked well, with 400 people signing up for the treatment in 1994, 1,000 people in 1996, and since then, the amount of people in the program has been stable at about 1,500. The empathetic, people-centered

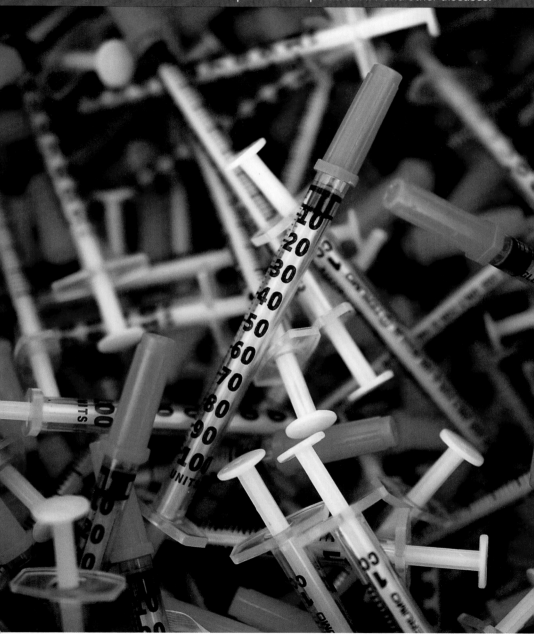

The unconventional needle-exchange program allows addicts to trade in used needles for clean ones to prevent the spread of HIV and other diseases.

approach to treatment has seen fewer new cases of heroin use in Switzerland—in 2005, there were between 100 and 150 new cases, while in 2012 there were 37 new people entering into the program. Additionally, heroin-related deaths have decreased 50 percent.

The program is not a place to go and do drugs. Rather, it is a place that allows the heroin addict some control over their lives, eventually allowing them to leave the program when they are comfortable and feel ready to—50 percent stay in the program for at least 2 years, while only 20 percent stay for longer than 15 years.

Other countries have seen the success of supervised injection facilities and have opened their own to help handle the epidemic. The first legal supervised injection facility in North America is in Vancouver, Canada. A heroin user obtains drugs before coming in, and the facility provides clean equipment, including syringes and cooking materials, to prevent the spread of diseases. Additionally, the facility has nurses on site at all times to handle any overdoses immediately, and between 2015 and 2016, out of more than 3 million visits, there were "4,922 overdose interventions without any deaths."[50] What is unique about the facility is there is also a detox doctor on site for when the user is ready to get clean. The facility does not push the user to use these services, yet the demand to see the doctor is such that the facility cannot keep up. "One thing that is unique to supervised injection facilities is their ability to coax some of the city's most difficult-to-reach drug users into seeing a doctor … or even to try detox. Insite users are 30 percent more likely to go to addiction treatment programs."[51]

The United States has not adopted the policies of countries such as Switzerland, and supervised injection facilities have yet to be installed. However, cities such as Ithaca, New York, and Seattle, Washington, have made proposals to have their own facilities set up. This plan also created a lot of backlash, with opponents saying that it removes the stigma from using heroin, which means it is not perceived as dangerous. Others believe that it is just what is needed—removing some of the danger from the allure of heroin may make it not seem as appealing.

Safe injection facilities provide drug materials such as these for addicts to use heroin in a supervised setting. Safe injection facilities are often the first step from chronic addiction to recovery.

STRATEGIES TO CONFRONT THE HEROIN EPIDEMIC

The heroin epidemic was a concern for Democratic presidential nominee Hillary Clinton in the 2016 U.S. presidential election. As Clinton traveled through states after announcing her run for president, voters voiced concerns about the heroin epidemic, which inspired her strategy to confront the epidemic:

My plan sets five goals: empower communities to prevent drug use among teenagers; ensure every person

Hillary Clinton is shown here listening to the story of a young woman recovering from heroin addiction.

suffering from addiction can obtain comprehensive treatment; ensure that all first responders carry naloxone, which can stop overdoses from becoming fatal; require health care providers to receive training in recognizing substance use disorders and to consult a prescription drug monitoring program before prescribing controlled substances; and prioritize treatment over prison for low-level and nonviolent drug offenders, so we can end the era of mass incarceration ... Through improved treatment, prevention, and training, we can end this quiet epidemic once and for all.[1]

1. Hillary Clinton, "Another View – Hillary Clinton: How We Can Win the Fight Against Substance Abuse," *Union Leader*, September 1, 2015. www.unionleader.com/article/20150901/OPINION02/150909909/1004/opinion.

The Future

In 2015, President Barack Obama instituted strategies to help end the heroin epidemic, starting with prescription painkillers. According to the new guidelines, "prescription painkillers should not be a first-choice for treating common ailments"[52] such as back pain. Instead, doctors should encourage patients "to try physical therapy, exercise and over-the-counter pain medications before turning to opioid painkillers for chronic pain." Additionally, "under the new guidelines, doctors would prescribe painkillers only after considering nonaddictive pain relievers, behavioral changes and other options. The CDC also wants doctors to prescribe the lowest effective dose possible."[53]

As the epidemic continues, officials are thinking of different ways to combat heroin use. Some states focus more on prosecuting for heroin when there is a death. Other states arrest for every small crime in the hope that it deters larger crimes, while another group of states pinpoint where exactly heroin is hitting them the hardest or where it is sold the most and focus on that area. The proportions of the recent epidemic have eliminated any previous ways of fighting heroin. After all, this epidemic is unprecedented, and more than a hundred users can die in one week in a community. The previous methods of tackling heroin use simply do not cut it anymore.

Additionally, parents that have lost children and do not wish for any other families to go through the pain they did are begging for any kind of help for heroin addicts. They want their child's death to bring about change in the world.

One prediction some have made for the future of the heroin epidemic is a vaccine. A heroin vaccine has been in the making for years; however, the success of the preclinical trials comes with a catch—pharmaceutical companies do not want to fund heroin trials. In trials on lab rats that were addicted to heroin, the vaccinated rats did not "relapse into addiction and were not hooked by high amounts of heroin in their system." The vaccine acts like a sponge: "If a person—or, in this case, rat—is inoculated, that 'sponge' sucks up the drug and prevents it from reaching the brain ... the heroin vaccine prevents the drug from reaching the brain at all."[54] Although many oppose a vaccine for heroin addiction and say that it only treats part of the addiction, it would still offer a chance for the user to turn their life around.

Most importantly, removing the stigma surrounding heroin addiction and not treating all addictions the same way is what is needed to move forward and save thousands of lives a year. Each person experiences addiction differently, and each person is addicted to heroin at a different level. Additionally, each person has different psychological reasons behind their addiction. Treating the individual with a person-centered approach and focusing on recovery is the start of reversing so many years of damage.

Notes

Introduction: Heroin: The Evolution of an Epidemic

1. "DEA Releases 2016 National Heroin Threat Assessment Summary," DEA, June 27, 2016. www.dea.gov/divisions/hq/2016/hq062716.shtml.
2. "Opium Throughout History," PBS *Frontline*. www.pbs.org/wgbh/pages/frontline/shows/heroin/etc/history.html.
3. "What is Public Health?," CDC Foundation. www.cdcfoundation.org/content/what-public-health.
4. Lindsey Cook, "The Heroin Epidemic, in 9 Graphs," *U.S. News & World Report*, August 19, 2015. www.usnews.com/news/blogs/data-mine/2015/08/19/the-heroin-epidemic-in-9-graphs.

Chapter One: Heroin's History

5. "Transforming Opium Poppies Into Heroin," PBS *Frontline*. www.pbs.org/wgbh/pages/frontline/shows/heroin/transform/.
6. "Transforming Opium Poppies Into Heroin."
7. "Opium Throughout History."
8. Alix Spiegel, "What Vietnam Taught Us About Breaking Bad Habits," NPR: *Your Health*, January 2, 2012. www.npr.org/sections/health-shots/2012/01/02/144431794/what-vietnam-taught-us-about-breaking-bad-habits.
9. Peter Kerr, "Growth in Heroin Use Ending as City Users Turn to Crack," *New York Times*, September 13, 1986. www.nytimes.com/1986/09/13/nyregion/growth-in-heroin-use-ending-as-city-users-turn-to-crack.html?pagewanted=all.
10. Edward Jay Epstein, *Agency of Fear: Opiates and Political Power in America*. London, UK: Verso, 1990, p. 24.
11. Epstein, *Agency of Fear: Opiates and Political Power in America*, p. 28.
12. Epstein, *Agency of Fear: Opiates and Political Power in America*, p. 28.

13. "The Truth About Heroin: International Statistics," Foundation for a Drug-Free World. www.drugfreeworld.org/drug-facts/heroin/international-statistics.html.
14. Susan Brink, "How Heroin Kills: What Might Have Happened to Philip Seymour Hoffman," *National Geographic*, February 4, 2014. news.nationalgeographic.com/news/2014/02/140204-philip-seymour-hoffman-actor-heroin-overdose/.
15. Susan Brink, "How Heroin Kills: What Might Have Happened to Philip Seymour Hoffman."

Chapter Two: The Effects of Heroin

16. Laura J. Martin, "Heroin: What You Need to Know," WebMD, May 1, 2016. www.webmd.com/mental-health/addiction/heroin-use.
17. Jen Christensen, "How Heroin Kills You," CNN, August 29, 2014. www.cnn.com/2014/02/04/health/how-heroin-kills/.
18. Brian Palmer, "Brain changes in an addict make it hard to resist heroin and similar drugs," *The Washington Post*, February 17, 2014. www.washingtonpost.com/national/health-science/brain-changes-in-an-addict-make-it-hard-to-resist-heroin-and-similar-drugs/2014/02/14/dcc91c5e-9366-11e3-84e1-27626c5ef5fb_story.html.
19. Deborah Condon, "Heroin Causes Alzheimer-like Brain Damage," IrishHealth, June 27, 2005. www.irishhealth.com/article.html?level=4&id=7759.
20. Carl Nierenberg, "10 Interesting Facts About Heroin," Live Science, October 27, 2016. www.livescience.com/56604-facts-about-heroin.html.
21. "What are the medical complications of chronic heroin use?," National Institute on Drug Abuse, November 2014. www.drugabuse.gov/publications/research-reports/heroin/what-are-medical-complications-chronic-heroin-use.
22. "What are the medical complications of chronic heroin use?."
23. Healthwise, "Repair of Nasal Septal Perforation – Surgery Overview," WebMD, November 14, 2014. www.webmd.com/

allergies/tc/repair-of-nasal-septal-perforation-surgery-overview.

24. Jason S. Hamilton, "Septal Perforation Brief Facts," Osborne Head & Neck Institute Division of Plastic Surgery. www.perforatedseptum.com/perforated-septum-treatment/.

25. Quoted in Rose Ciotta and Luke Moretti, "Region's heroin epidemic worsens," WIVB, September 30, 2015. wivb.com/2015/09/30/regions-heroin-epidemic-worsens/.

26. Brink, "How Heroin Kills: What Might Have Happened to Philip Seymour Hoffman."

27. Christensen, "How heroin kills you."

Chapter Three: The Trap of Addiction

28. Palmer, "Brain changes in an addict make it hard to resist heroin and similar drugs."

29. "Biology of Addiction: Drugs and Alcohol Can Hijack Your Brain," *NIH News in Health*, October 2015. newsinhealth.nih.gov/issue/oct2015/feature1.

30. "Biology of Addiction: Drugs and Alcohol Can Hijack Your Brain."

31. Kayla Smith, "Heroin Addiction and Abuse," Addiction Center, April 12, 2016. www.addictioncenter.com/drugs/heroin/.

32. "Heroin Use and Abuse: Side Effects: Treatment for Heroin Addiction," Project Know. www.projectknow.com/research/heroin-effects/.

33. "Treating Heroin Addiction," Project Know. www.projectknow.com/research/heroin/.

34. Erik MacLaren, "Post-Acute Withdrawal Syndrome," Drug Abuse.com. drugabuse.com/library/post-acute-withdrawal-syndrome/.

35. "FDA approves first buprenorphine implant for treatment of opioid dependence," U.S. Food & Drug Administration, May 26, 2016. www.fda.gov/NewsEvents/Newsroom/PressAnnouncements/ucm503719.htm.

36. "FDA approves first buprenorphine implant for treatment of opioid dependence."

Chapter Four: The Legality of Heroin

37. Keegan Hamilton, "The Golden Age of Drug Trafficking: How Meth, Cocaine, and Heroin Move Around the World," *Vice News*, April 25, 2016. news.vice.com/article/drug-trafficking-meth-cocaine-heroin-global-drug-smuggling.
38. "Drug Policy & History," DrugAbuse.net. www.drugabuse.net/drug-policy/.
39. "Drug Scheduling," United States Drug Enforcement Administration. www.dea.gov/druginfo/ds.shtml.
40. Quoted in Scott Pelley, "A New Direction on Drugs," CBS *60 Minutes*, June 5, 2016. www.cbsnews.com/news/60-minutes-a-new-direction-on-drugs-2/.
41. Quoted in Pelley, "A New Direction on Drugs."
42. Melissa Locker, "Heroin Epidemic's New Terror: Carfentanil," *Rolling Stone*, September 8, 2016. www.rollingstone.com/culture/news/heroin-epidemics-new-terror-carfentanil-w438712.
43. Locker, "Heroin Epidemic's New Terror: Carfentanil."
44. Andrew Blankstein, "Pink: Stronger Than Heroin, but Legal in Most States," NBC News, October 15, 2016. www.nbcnews.com/storyline/americas-heroin-epidemic/pink-stronger-heroin-legal-most-states-n666446.

Chapter Five: Tackling the Epidemic

45. Katharine Q. Seelye, "Heroin Epidemic Increasingly Seeps Into Public View," *New York Times*, March 6, 2016. www.nytimes.com/2016/03/07/us/heroin-epidemic-increasingly-seeps-into-public-view.html?_r=0.
46. Gina Kolata and Sarah Cohen, "Drug Overdoses Propel Rise in Mortality Rates of Young Whites," *New York Times*, January 16, 2016. www.nytimes.com/2016/01/17/science/drug-overdoses-propel-rise-in-mortality-rates-of-young-whites.html.
47. Kolata and Cohen, "Drug Overdoses Propel Rise in Mortality Rates of Young Whites."
48. "Fact Sheet: Obama Administration Announces Public and Private Sector Efforts to Address Prescription Drug Abuse and Heroin Use," The White House, October 21, 2015. www.whitehouse.

gov/the-press-office/2015/10/21/fact-sheet-obama-adminis-
tration-announces-public-and-private-sector.

49. "Today's Heroin Epidemic," Centers for Disease Control and
Prevention, July 7, 2015. www.cdc.gov/vitalsigns/heroin/
index.html.

50. "User Statistics: Statistics and Facts from 2015/2016," Vancouver Coastal Health. www.vch.ca/your-health/health-
topics/supervised-injection/user-statistics/.

51. Francie Diep, "Inside North America's Only Legal Safe
Injection Facility," *Pacific Standard*, August 30, 2016.
psmag.com/inside-north-americas-only-legal-safe-injection-
facility-7fc82a6af8f5#.qjxzwz5r9.

52. CBS/AP, "New Guidelines Aim to Reduce Epidemic of Opioid
Painkiller Abuse," CBS News, March 15, 2016. www.cbsnews.
com/news/opioid-painkiller-guidelines/.

53. CBS/AP, "New Guidelines Aim to Reduce Epidemic of Opioid
Painkiller Abuse."

54. Alexandra Sifferlin, "Why You've Never Heard of the Vaccine for Heroin Addiction," *TIME*, January 9, 2015.
time.com/3654784/why-youve-never-heard-of-the-vaccine-
for-heroin-addiction/.

Narconon
7065 Hollywood Boulevard
Los Angeles, CA 90028
(800) 775-8750
www.narconon.org
This organization provides information on drugs, including history, effects, and treatment. Additionally, the organization is a rehab program with facilities around the world. They are available to talk 24 hours a day if you or someone you know has a drug addiction.

National Institute on Drug Abuse (NIDA)
6001 Executive Boulevard
Room 5213
Bethesda, MD 20892
(301) 443-1124
www.nida.nih.gov
NIDA is one of the leading organizations supporting research on drug abuse and addiction. The website features updated scientific information and research on various drugs such as heroin and also provides information on treatments.

Police Assisted Addiction and Recovery Initiative (PAARI)
One Bridge StreetSuite 300
Newton, MA 02458
info@paariusa.org
paariusa.org
PAARI works with addicts and focuses on recovery rather than punishment for crimes. This program connects addicts with appropriate treatment facilities and programs, no matter where they live.

SMART Recovery
7304 Mentor Avenue
Suite F
Mentor, Ohio 44060
(440) 951-5357
www.smartrecovery.org
This program provides information on drugs and is targeted toward helping teens with substance abuse disorders get their lives back. The program has an online community, has multiple rehabilitation centers, and can be contacted through its national office or a local office.

Substance Abuse and Mental Health Services Administration (SAMHSA)
5600 Fishers Lane
Rockville, MD 20857
(877) 726-4727
www.samhsa.gov
SAMHSA is focused on treatment. It provides an overview of specific drugs, as well as information on how a user can get help and get their life back on track. The toll-free hotline is confidential.

Books

Brezina, Corona. *Alcohol and Drug Offenses: Your Legal Rights.* New York, NY: Rosen Publishing, 2015.
This book goes into detail regarding different penalties for various drugs and alcohol when a teenager is at the center of the crime. The book also offers advice on how to stay away from this type of trouble.

Esherick, Joan. *Drug- & Alcohol-Related Health Issues.* Broomall, PA: Mason Crest Publishers, 2014.
Created for teenagers, this book presents an overview of all drugs, including heroin, to help young people get the facts before possibly being confronted with them.

Parks, Peggy J. *The Dangers of Painkillers.* San Diego, CA: ReferencePoint Press, 2017.
This book presents an in-depth view of painkillers, which is often where heroin addiction begins. The book discusses the problem, effects, treatment, and more.

Sanna, E.J. *Heroin and Other Opioids: Poppies' Perilous Children.* Philadelphia, PA: Mason Crest Publishers, 2008.
This book focuses on all opioids—from opium to codeine to heroin—and discusses the history, dangers, and treatment of addiction to these drugs.

Sonder, Ben. *All About Heroin.* New York, NY: Franklin Watts, 2002.
This book provides further study into heroin and also examines the lifestyles of users and government responses to heroin.

Websites

Drug Enforcement Administration (DEA)
www.dea.gov
  The DEA is the organization charged with enforcing drug laws
  and developing antidrug programs in the United States. The
  website contains information about drugs and drug policy, as well
  as punishment at the federal level.

Heroin Is Not Chic
www.heroinisnotchic.com
  This nonprofit organization promotes awareness of the heroin
  epidemic and brings attention to the glamorization of the heroin
  look in fashion in an effort to combat the popularity of the look.

Just Think Twice
www.justthinktwice.gov
  This website for teens has fact sheets about various drugs,
  including heroin. Also on the website are informative videos,
  true stories, and information about the effects various drugs have
  on the body.

National Institute on Drug Abuse for Teens
teens.drugabuse.gov
  This website provides information on different types of drugs,
  especially heroin. There are informative articles on the various
  effects of heroin, an educational blog, and games to explore the
  brain and your drug knowledge.

Office of National Drug Control Policy
www.whitehousedrugpolicy.gov
  This office is charged with establishing policies, priorities, and
  objectives for the drug control program of the United States.
  On the website is information about treatment, as well as the
  policies the U.S. president creates involving the drug policy.

Nicole Horning has written a number of books for children. She holds a bachelor's degree in English and a master's degree in education from D'Youville College in Buffalo, New York. She lives in Western New York with her cats and writes and reads in her free time.